Dedicated to all of my students, particularly the one who found my tying of shoes alluring.

2

July 2019: 10 months from retirement

My friend John "the Nez" Nesbitt said the other day that his job was to leave a record of his trek on this planet. He has lived a life that surely deserves to be remembered. Regarding me, that could be heard as a bit egocentric, as it assumes someone might want to read such a thing. There is another function for writing: to enact memory. Also to replace it when it fails. Already the twinkles of details lost occur enough to prompt me: "You will not forever remember these things, so write them down. Do it now."

Here in 2019, many of the things I recall about teaching since 1980 are likely to be inaccurate as to particulars. But there is solace in knowing that no one knows as much about what I've experienced as I do[*], so if anyone is qualified to write it up, it's me.

Leaving aside, then, the existential morass of "why write at all," which every teacher explores each time there are papers to grade, I proceed, to wit:

[*]hats off to HD Thoreau

First Day, Austin Texas

The first day seems like the right place to start, though many days prior to August 25 of 1980 might easily be as relevant to my teaching life.

My ground-level apartment was small but dry, except for what the roaches left behind. It was a good place to sleep through the night and wake relieved to be alive, about 6 miles north of Austin's University of Texas campus.

The 7 story campus building I was to appear in at 8am was called something else back then, but now it is the Jesse H. Jones Communication Center. First floor, room __, first day. Solo teaching, to be observed by an allergy-stricken yet august professor, one of two such observations that occurred, as I recall, over a 1.5 year period. The night before, everything was made ready. My thoughts, my clothes, my notes, my Snoopy windup alarm clock (a well-meaning gag-gift, but no less annoying.) All set. Alarm, 6:45, which seemed early back then but today seems like sleeping in. All set. I slept with the window open, cool soft Texas night air creeping over the parking lot through the screen. I'd never thought as much as that night about how thin screens are, and how easily one could be removed. But once asleep, I slept well.

Awakened not by the alarm but by its absence, I sat up in a panic and looked at Snoopy. 7:45! The sun through the window was already Texas hot. Here I was sitting swaddled and no doubt

4

my students were already assembling under their first day hangover for delivery of the product at 8am. Things were said in the apartment that would not be polite to repeat this early in my testimony.

By 7:50 I was riding like a madman on my ancient Honda, breaking lots of rules of sense, my career in the balance, my ass barely. Helmet, t-shirt, cutoffs, shoes that matched the ensemble, I rode clad in purpose and panic...purpic. Screw the parking regulations, which I had meant to review in leisure at my desk upon arrival. The bike got left under an eave near a staircase; that's all I remember.

I tore up the stairs, helmet banging my bare legs, crossed the lobby like an Illinois wind, thanking God I'd memorized the room number. I saw the light of the open door, and people beginning to stand up as the apologetic back of the supervising Professor C. was saying something about Wednesday.

"Stop!" I called from the door, tossing my helmet like a bowling ball into a corner. "I'm here!"

Hardly the rhetorically bejeweled opening I'd planned. Professor C. turned to me, smiled chuckling and said, "Well!"

From there my hand touched the chalk, my mouth opened, and whatever fate was to be worked upon the American Collegiate System (and numerous international students) for the next 4 decades had begun. As for what I knew that qualified me to be teaching that class, that day, or any day, one can say only this: not much. But knowing not much is not a problem if one can follow the advice of Isaac Stern, who is reported to have said something along these lines: "What can be taught about playing violin can be taught in ten minutes. The rest is added to continue being paid for lessons." I've been getting paid for "giving lessons" ever since. Then I was 21. Now I'm nearly 61 and less than a year from retirement, four schools and thousands of students later. That's a long lesson, and it started late, in a panic, out of breath, poorly dressed, and filled with wonder at the miracle that I'd been allowed to teach in the first place.

From that day on I've been in a constant panic about being late and, to my recollection, I have only been late about 5 times, give or take, and only once late enough that students had started to leave as I flew into the room. Whether being on time is a virtue or not, it has been an example and, for that, I duly thank myself on their behalf.

Excursion: "being an example"

There are myths and legends and lies about how hallowed teachers once were, loved (mainly in old movies), respected, honored, emulated. What a bunch of crap.

Still there lives a thread of expectation, sometimes today only evident when a teacher dares to be impolite, that teachers set an example. Whatever the subject that is taught, the teaching of it is expected to be communicative of exemplary speech and thought. Is this realistic? Is it perhaps a bit egoistic, to think: "I am exemplary."

But we are, in function if not in form.

The math prof is to be exemplary in doing math but also in teaching it. And that includes showing up on time.

To get to the original thread that started this excursus: the basics are a chance for teachers to demonstrate what is exemplary, so here below they are (and these are hard to do all of the time, but doing them most of the time may be remarkable enough) :

Be on time.
Meet deadlines.
"Don't write a check with your mouth that your ass can't cash." (Clinton J___, Hampton)
Stay until the end.
Have energy, but don't rush.
Shut up when someone else is talking.
Talk with people more than to them or at them.
Lecture well, and screw the people who think it's backward. They need a lecture.
Don't use 10 words when 1 will do.
Speak plainly.
Be brief.
Dress acceptably, and
Don't sport a wristwatch or evening wear.

***

The Mouth

One of the few dangers in teaching (added to being shot or having one's legs broken for giving a bad grade) is getting too comfortable. Comfort, normally a good thing in public speaking (of which teaching is a subspecies), can lead to casualness, an ease which reduces filtering of thought on its way to The Mouth. And lo! the comfort of the teacher is just one half of the volatile mixture; the other half is the comfort of the students in listening, as they come to have expectations, usually erroneous and possibly inflated, born of the good behavior most teachers demonstrate early in a course. They relax, ready to listen, knowing what to expect. This can lead to shocks if The Mouth lapses into unfiltration, as mine once did while I was teaching as a TA in Texas at UT Austin...

This isn't a long story, but being short might make the point, as transitions from one state (of mind and body) can happen quickly, as I found out the first time The Mouth almost crashed the plane, so early in my tender career.

The course was Intro to Speech Communication or Public Speaking or one of those "basic courses" in General Education (of which we may have something to say later*) that everyone was required to take. We were a few weeks in, and thus Persuasion had quite naturally come up as a relevant topic upon which to expound. In any case, my excursus led quickly to the 20th century's most

8

skilled persuaders, the Nazi's, for whom no one has love (except maybe ex-Nazi's who muse over how much fun they had). As I warmed up to a description of their persuasive propaganda, the pace quickened. Students had seen movies, some had even read books, and nearly all of them way back when knew a fair bit about the size and the gravity of the Second European War that Spread Like Crazy. Anyhow, I was looking at each student as often as possible along the way, controlling for the natural and yet unacceptable tendency to look at the females more often (as I was just a few years older than many, and nearly the same age as some.) One student, whose name now is lost to me (all the better), had displayed unusual attention throughout the opening weeks of the class, and appeared to have accepted me as Someone Safe To Listen To. She was looking and listening, as out of The Mouth came, "....those motherf--" Now, there was a full stop, and any umpire would have called it a legal swing check, but as there is no ambiguity on which word or part-of-word remained unspoken, no way to see how that might have been the start of another descriptive phrase, "motherfuckers" hung in the air like a septic cloud, for just a split second. Perhaps I'm extrapolating, for then I saw nothing but the transformation of her face from pink and attentive to gray and fallen, as if she had died and decayed half a day's worth in half a second. I knew there was no recall, recovery, apology, or acknowledgement that could make things any less bad, forget better. I moved on, unpunished, not a word spoken from anyone, not a look telling if the others did notice or gave a shit.

*General Ed was supposed to happen from K-12. Why does it persist? \$\$

I never forgot that change, and the lesson taught by her face to The Mouth: in the space of a syllable it can all be lost: trust, attention, even learning. Offense, yes. Beyond that, her face signaled disappointment so deep it changed how her blood flowed. Oh fuck, I thought then and wondered many a time since: When will I fail to stop at the "f?"

Since that motherfucking* day, my filter has been on strong. A professor that roared in the 80's and 90's is now likely to be called a maniac or worse. "Content delivery" having replaced education in practice if not in fact (due to web teaching), passion and emotion must be dialed way down, way, way down. Nothing louder than a cellphone, please.

*such a nasty term, but alternatives such as puppyfucking just don't have the cultural gravitas.

Other Things I have to Remember to Remember:
- ☐ The Standing Ovation of Felons
- ☐ Passing Out
- ☐ Puking
- ☐ Seizures
- ☐ Letting Loose for fun and why it's No Longer Cool
- ☐ Guest Speakers
- ☐ Exams

10

- ☐ First Grade
- ☐ The Necessary Evil of the Illusion of Arbitrariness (sic)
- ☐ Expertise (and getting the book days before)
- ☐ The Book (yeah, Marvin)
- ☐ Obsolescence
- ☐ Changing the Names of Things (for sport and profit)
- ☐ Costs
- ☐ Singing to Start Class
- ☐ Douchebag and Richard

Bring Real Life In (fake as it is)   Better make a note on this one. Nothing seems to perk up a class, whether it be in Texas, Virginia, Illinois, New York, or Kentucky, like a good recording of real people really communicating. Audio or video or both, students get into it, especially if the recording is an interaction involving conflict. There's some rubbernecking going on, and some of the ancient allure of drama operating, but for whatever reason, we do it because it works. But what does it work to do? The exemplars we choose, like this or that voicemail, or conversations in a car or outside a Dairy Queen, are snippets, real as a photograph. And as fake as one. A photo can show a slice of light, shorter than any seeing eye can apprehend, and thus grab for attention and lingering gazes what in reality never was appreciable that way. A real unreal thing. And so with the snippets of video we bring in, old speeches, news clips, interviews,

Robert Frost reading a poem, voicemails: they are the *capta* of communication, but they are not *it*. We must artificialize communications in order to study them. We do this. I have done this and do it more than ever now that media are so easily shared.
People love a story.
More things I need to remember to remember:
- ☐ First Days
- ☐ Exemplary Teachers who Taught By Teaching
- ☐ Drunks and other Lecturers Who Made College Great
- ☐ Paul Hurley (on teaching what NOT to do...) how perfect was his name, b/c he made ya wanna.
- ☐ Hampton: all the tales and the fails. Most remarkably (circa 1983) b/c less predictable (I've got a normally sized head as far as I know), a student wrote anonymously on a course evaluation that I had "a big forehead." That's an oddly precise insult, and maybe wasn't an insult at all but rather a comparative observation. Therefore, I started thinking about the class roster, scanning my semi-photographic memory (the other half is pornographic) for students who had small foreheads who, logically, would find mine oversized in comparison. The student was nice not to call me a racist or anything serious, but I noticed it then and

12

I remember it now as one of the most
ambiguous, but presumably insulting things,
particularly because it preceded what has
become a significant recession of the front
line of my mop.

The Guitar
The year 1986 was the first time I played
guitar in class as a teacher. A General Education
section of Public Speaking, a night class,
Carbondale Illinois, SIU. For some reason I had my
case and axe in hand, and set them in the corner
before class. At the time roll would normally have
been called, a student said, "play something." Why
not?
Can't recall now which tune it was.
Probably *For What It's Worth* (What's that sound?)
I was not nervous to play, but chose not to look at
the audience, which to me makes the most sense
unless one is singing to them, which I was not. I
played and sang in front of them, and they could
listen or not. I cared not a whit. But I noticed
something about the class that evening, compared to
the normal opening (hello, roll call, where were
we?...) The class seemed odd, like it had tipped
toward a new place, a new air, or aire, one might
say, which I just did.
I don't think I played again, because I had
only one guitar and I wasn't going to be toting it
back and forth to campus on my bicycle
ferchrissakes. Still, the memory of the change to

the class, an evening class at that, lingered. When I got to Alfred University, I started my 4 years there with a song, and played every day in class unless time was at a premium and the students were performing (speeches or pieces or whatever). The Texas songs of Larry Browning and Bob Hopper repertoire were the mainstay, which had the advantage of being so quaint as to be generally unknown to students; thus my performance had to be judged compared to nothing. Incomparable, yes, but not in the usual sense. I mixed in original songs, tried out new tunes, and they had no way of knowing which was which, written or stolen, unless they snuck a glance at the list taped to the back of my guitar.

Some classes clap; others don't. I play anyway. Some clap for a few days, then trail off to nothing, and no one starts it up again. I play anyway. When I don't play for a day, the classes where no one claps have the same number of people complain as those that do clap. Clapter is not an indication of success. Maybe some clap because they're afraid not to, afraid that this crazy fuck who plays *musica obscurata* might bust them on grades for not browning up. That's one reason I never look at anyone during or after the song.

In 2019, for the first time I can recall since 1987, a student asked in class why I play. I said I'm not sure, told the brief tale of Carbondale and having the case with me, and said mainly that there is no reason not to, excusing the grammar. He

14

remained slightly confused looking. I do believe
I'm as old as his grandpa now, which may add to the
confusion, since I play a coupla Pink Floyd and
know all the words.

The Gap
        Speaking of grandpa, I am now easily as old
as the grandfathers of some of my students, which
brings to mind The Gap. The Gap is that age-space
between one's students and oneself. On that fateful
day my Snoopy alarm clock didn't go off, I was still
a bit of 21. Many of my students were within 3
years of my age, some of them the same. And for
many years there were students who were older than
I. The Gap is not just an observation of age
statistics, however, it is a rhetorical and cultural
standpoint (age is), and spaces between ages qualify
or disqualify many things. The "closeness" in age
can engender a familiarity, a rhetorical basis for
saying "us, we, our" without exaggeration.
        There is more to The Gap than a mere
difference in age, for there is what that age
difference means to shared ground. This
"generation gap" affects families differently, as
families may not be in the habit of exploring topics
in depth quite the way we do in classes. Teachers,
using the technique of starting in a familiar place
and moving into an unfamiliar one, like to use
exempla, shared stories, moments, common
knowledge, as it were. This is where The Gap can
become a problem.

I used to be able to refer to Holden Caulfield, *Good Country People* and Cap'n Ahab with confidence my students would get the allusions. This is a sign of the widening Gap, as today few or none will know, and if one does, it might be from catching *Moby Dick* on video. But Holden? Forget it. Maybe that is good, since he was a crabby bore who made being a miserable geek seem very cool for a while. Shame is that, as Holden and Ahab have gone the way of the dodo, what is left in their place? Nothing. No shared stories, except maybe from a television series, a recent movie, or scripture. This diversification and oversupply have ruined both of those traditional troughs as well. Just last semester I alluded to "jousting with windmills," and no one knew what was up, so I asked if anyone knew of Don Quixote, and no one did. I said, "no problem, not everyone can know every story." Yet what a bummer. I guess they'd be just as surprised I have never heard Lady Gaga "sing." The man of LaMancha is now what dude from where? Yes, it was a ridiculous story, but the windmills thing was cool. Quixotic loses its boom.

What Am I Doing?

I am a speech teacher, put most tersely. How this happened we'll get to later.

Keep this in mind when appreciating my predicament. Math can be done perfectly; that is probably the only worthwhile way to do it. Not so with speech. People don't get together as math amateurs and have a math jam where they enjoy getting most of the digits right. But speakers and musicians DO jam, and no matter how awesome any given jam might be, planned or otherwise, no jam is perfect. Perfection may not even be the goal, might be boring in the end. In math, perfection is everything. Now, on to speech. We are in an odd and oddly quaint predicament, we teachers of speech. As one of the clan, I have spotted several pragmatic paradoxes:

- We teach a thing we can never do to perfection
- We are certain about our theories, but our theories are not certainties.
- We are purporting to teach (in college no less) people about something they've been doing since before they could walk
- The situations (speaking contexts some say) about which we teach are always historic; everything else is a prediction
- Our subject is not widely loved (to say the least)*
- To teach speech and to be weak in its practice is every bit as hazardous as a math teacher who cannot add, except that in speech communication we teach "individual traits" as religious icons, and often excuse incompetence under a banner of "style."

- Style, in other words, is ever what and whatever we teach in speech
- We've argued for decades that we are "more than public speaking." However, that phrase precisely depicts what we study and do. (Add a "the" before public and it continues to make the point.)
- The Gap becomes more evident and obstaculating because speech is made of contemporaneous meaning and, as noted elsewhere in this wander of words, meanings come and go and change so often that one person cannot spend decades teaching about meaning without adding and deleting constantly from the *Fund of Exempla.*
- I facilitate lessons in manners and practices that I do not myself always follow. But is this any less than the former sinner talking about overcoming sin?
- If sin is, and is kept only, to mean "missing the mark," then we all do, and frequently enough that the trick we teach might be how to fuck up in an entertaining or otherwise useful way.
- We disdain lecturing and deliver long talks on the subject.
- We want our students to be good enough for us to polish, but not so horrid as to need a coarse bastard file.

18

Speaking of coarse bastards, there was once an MSU student named Charles Albright. I use his name now because he is deceased and will care slightly less than he might have while alive. He would be thrilled. He was as old as Satan, looking back at 80, claimed to have been L. Ron Hubbard's bodyguard, walked bent like a thick vine limb wrapping itself around a leaned over tree, and had either no filters whatsoever or a good set that he just chose not to use. In any case, he could fill a room with a range of unpleasant odours (sic), all in the human ooze category. Even his breath could be buttered. That's how yeasty he was. But he was a great writer and came to classes because he could for free at MSU in KY and to remind the world that he existed.

One day in class, whilst students were delivering public speeches, a young lady of notable proportions, wearing soccer gear for before or after class, delivered her serious talk on how to manage a difficult illness. Mr. Albright, age circa 80, (aka Colonel Albright, Dr. Albright, and just Albright), who had his perch on the front row of tables, opened the Comments period by saying, "You look fantastic in those shorts." This was about 2014, so the world had not gone completely insane yet about "hair-ess-ment" and was still capable of forgiving Old People for being boorish fuckheads.

"Thank you," the more mature 19 year old woman said as she headed for her seat in the back row, a place she no doubt chose so as NOT to be looked at, if one might speculate.

"And your speech was engaging, too," Albright continued, not the least bit ogley or lasciviously. I invited further comments from the class, and there were some stammerings that redirected, but the cloud of his forwardness hung like a fart, Albright being Albright, and old, and smelly, so that I knew I'd have to do a follow up.

Only once or twice have I done formal follow ups in the years since 1980, to address what occurred during a class meeting. I contacted this student using email and asked her if she felt as if anything needed to be done following the comments in class. She briefly replied No, and wrote as if she noticed what he said but cared nothing as to its significance. Ahhhh, Bach.

I never did talk to Albright about that, maybe because he once said that I was one of the few at MSU he could understand, due to his highly fucked up hearing, and I'd have hated to stain that potential should it ever be necessary to really get through to him as his star fell. That's not heroic. That's conceited of me because he really was a magnificent character and a bodacious writer.

Albright raised hell wherever he went, and qualifies as the only student I've known that was

20

formally, permanently banned from campus and
university functions. Good job, Colonel! Not
worth saying why, but let's just sum it up by noting
that people don't like being forced to give what they
promise quite as often as Charles Albright
demanded it be given.

The Example
Teaching in prison was one of the highlights
of my career, but only in retrospect. During the
semesters I went inside, very few were the moments
of enjoyment or appreciation, though there were
enough and the money was good. The guards were
bigger assholes than the prisoners, in most cases.
None of the prisoners I worked with were assholes,
come to think, at least not to me. None of the
keepers seemed pleased to see college being
provided to the inmates. I can see why; most of
them could not afford college on the pay they
earned taking care of men who were getting it for
free. A felony seemed like a smarter career choice,
considering the role of higher education. But the
prisoners who went to school were very few out of
the total population, and it was a privilege hard to
earn and easy to lose.
An evening course I taught in Business and
Professional Speech (don't laugh, you knower), had
a variety of gentlemen in attendance. The ones who
sat in the back were of particular interest. I did not
study any of them closely while they were at a
distance, but when they approached the desk, I had

a chance to notice a thing or two. First, hygiene seemed to be very important to everyone. Makes sense in prison. One stinker could ruin everyone's day. Second, tattoos were popular, even though this was just the mid-90's.

One of the more captivating tattoos was really a set of 10, working hand in hand, you might say. The gentleman, who's name I cannot recall and whose crime I never knew, came to the front to submit a page of work, placed it flat on the desk and slid it toward me with both hands, *a la* da Vinci smoothing a sketch. His palms faced downward, and his fingers were spread so that the tops of all 10 were visible. The letters written on them were hard to miss, as they were angled to face forward to the reader rather than back to the man:

W H I T E   P O W E R, they read.

Great.

I said thank you and pretended not to notice his digital speech, offering the same calm, half smile/half grimace that I provided with equal measure to all residents. This same gentleman, either later that evening or in a subsequent class meeting (I am already forgetting details, but hey it was 25 years ago), spoke up during a discussion for the first time, offering an evocative example showing rhetorical sensitivity to his audience. The subject was Being Prepared for any eventuality during a presentation, so such things as a tech failure, or forgetting notes, were brought up. The principle was recommended: "have a backup plan."

22

White Power raised one of his lettered hands for the first time all term.

"Yeah, be prepared," he said. "Like when you go out on a job, take some extra ammo in case you run into the law."

Several fellow incarcerants nodded in knowing agreement. One or two rolled their eyes. (They were probably the ones in for shooting at trespassers or federal agents. Robbery was as alien to them as it was to me (officially.))

When a student speaks up, my axiom kicks in: thank them for contributing. I said, "A very practical example," and moved on to the next question.

Ahhhh, culture.

The Subject

Once a student complained about me to a mutual acquaintance because I "wasted time doing things not related to the subject." The subject of the course was Voice & Articulation, and I opened each class, after the song, with "dictionary time." After all, what are we voicing and articulating but words? And where can we find interesting tales about words? Right. But somehow he missed all that, and seems to have fumed through dictionary time, waiting for class to start.

Another interesting dictionary moment (we are in a small town on a small campus here, keep in mind) happened during the time students were invited to inquire about words they'd heard but did not understand, or had been arguing about. Up til this time, this went off without a problem, and some very interesting and occasionally arcane language got discussed. One day, during the period of my divorce, which was early 1997, a student in the back row, one of the Theatre gang who often seemed to resent me for some reason, despite my great empathy for their field's madness, raised his hand. My now-ex had been going out for salad, one might say (in line with "the salad days of youth"), fucking who knows who. This news gets around, as she did. So, the aforementioned student raises his hand and says,

"Yes, I've got a word: cuckold."

This word was familiar to me but not defined with certainty, so I looked it up. The room had grown very quiet, but I notice that now only in reflection. The usually boisterous back row was as silent as Catholics pretending to attend to a sermon.

I quickly found the definition; for to me the dictionary is pleasant and familiar territory...

"Oh..." I read the definition aloud and looked directly at him while finishing. There may have been a bit of a glare, not sure. But he reacted as if there were, and I asked. "Where did you come across that word?"

He paused, either recalling or composing.

"In a script," he said, as if deciding on a flavor of ice cream.

Now, you might think I was being paranoid, and I even thought that same thing almost instantly, for his explanation was more probable than him choosing to poke the eye of the Cyclops. But what confirmed his malintent for me was that he never came back to class after that.

I must have glared. Ooops.

Musings

- A dictionary is not a rule book. It is a recording of what people *used* to do, and might accurately reflect some of what they're still doing. It is used as a rulebook and as a doorstop with equal effect.
- (do not write in this space)

July 18, 2019

Today I write about today and how yesterday affects and effects it.

Never having considered myself a legitimate professor, the current contemplation of the approaching day when I will shift from professor to former is savored with a different flavor than it might be for true blue profs.

There are people who, if asked what I was to them, would answer, "my professor." And institutionally, historically, this would be accurate. They can call me their professor, as I call Dr. Marvin Kleinau my professor. In contrast to the title, though, isn't merely a chapter in the Impostor Syndrome, but rather a plain fact: I was never truly into it.

I did it.

I got paid for it.

On occasion someone learned something.

And that something might have a facet or feature unique to me. But doubtful.

I passed things along: the book, the message, the policy, the principle, the tradition, the history, the stories, axia and fabrications posing as examples, lengthy circumlocutions about being brief, quotes real, quotes fabricated (those were so much better)--all of this I passed along. In later years, the progenitors of online teaching would call classes the product and the operation "content delivery."

Lots of content, even in speech communication, confabulates a subject that probably grabs people at first as if they were taking a class in walking or breathing.

And they are.

So, what did I deliver in the way of Facts, Values, and Policies?Nothing consistently. Lots now and then.

Facts I knew and taught came mostly from Linguistics, the clinical side and the descriptive/prescriptive side. An alphabet for writing sounds (not a-phonetic letters like our normal alphabet) helped to create factual descriptions of the way people talk. I taught that alphabet. People used it. It was useful, the IPA. It stood still. But even that, even something so concrete as a writing system--the longer one looked at it and learned about its origins, forms, and consequences*--the fuzzier it became because of individual differences and preferences.

Other facts had to do with speech and the body, and could be proven or questioned by anyone who cared to compare themselves to the anatomical assertions of the charts and films. This was factual and useful to those who wished to learn how to command their speaking selves rather than be commanded by them. Everyone else just found it something to learn for the test, I suppose.

So and so said thus and so in this place at this time to these people in this way--these appear to be factual assertions, and when backed up by recordings take on the aspect of unequivocal truth. Still, recordings can be modified, and contextualization means a lot when the listeners are encountering a speech for the first time.

*this triumvirate borrowed from Otto Jespersen or William James, I think.

July 26, 2019

An easy way to dismiss the gravity of stopping my activity in the "professoriate" is to minimize the impact it did, does, and could have. "It" being teaching, of course. All one need do is reflect on the empty suits, the jaded, the tired, the poor, the misplaced professors whom one has had, and say, "they harmed me but little, so the damage I have done could not be any worse."

Sometimes the shitty ones were an inspiration. I certainly remember them every bit as well as the "competent."

Remember, Dear Reader, that I was generally a student of The Humanities, which means that while there were right answers, they were right answers about guesses people made.

Damage? "Do no harm" is the physician's pledge. Does the professor take a similar oath?

No.

We are not really qualified as teachers, technically speaking, as we are the only teachers

in K-16 who are not "certified" with licensure.
Oddly, I can teach college, university graduate
courses and teach teachers-to-be, but I could not
be employed to teach the first grade.
Kindergarten might have me as a guest speaker
but that's it. No public school system would, or
could, hire me as a teacher.

Where do people get teaching certificates?
At universities where 95% of the professors are
not certified to teach even the first grade.

What more can be said of this but that we
are insane?

Anyhow, this rant started as a worry about
how much what I've done has mattered, and thus
how much me stopping it will matter.

I must remember that Bertrand Russell
retired. Alfred North Whitehead retired. Even
Einstein retired. And the "academy" went on.
No one is indispensable.

I never worked to become indispensable, so
not being it is hardly a failure. A more noble
and realistic goal would be to have done no
harm, as more specifically, as Dr. Minor
paraphrased Wieman, "do not teach them
anything they will have to unlearn later."

Another problem arises with my teaching of
my subject: speech communication. Unlike
math, which does not bear in any immediately
obvious way on most of life's questions, speech
does very much matter every day in almost

every situation. Even hermits talk to themselves (or so I've heard...)

So, what then, is NOT in the view of the speech teacher? Every tussle, argument, dialectic, rhetorical campaign, every knick knack and paddy-whack, every doggy's bone, all of it is speech communication's business. This makes our subject at once about everything and, therefore, about nothing at all. It is too big to be appertained, so all teaching about it and of it is tragically flawed from the start with the ugly tumor of insufficiency, partiality, and the undeserved waft of sloth due to these shortages, or shortnesses, rather.

Anyway, some students along the road have said they learned something. Others no doubt did not realize they had until much later, and still others remember not a minute, not a fragment, not a second of my class, and that is OK. I've had good teachers I've forgotten and bad ones I remember. Being remembered is not always the highest form of praise. Being comfortably forgotten, but having perhaps placed some tile in the grand mosaic of another's life, *that* is satisfying in the abstract.

But not even close to as satisfying as getting paid.

Standing Ovation of Felons

One cannot be certain if everyone in an audience is a felon, even in prison. Some are there for other reasons, and some are there despite being innocent. Still, it's a fair wager that most of one's audience in a college class being taught in a medium security penitentiary are of the felonious category.

No human is a felon. Their actions have been felonious at times, though.

I'd been teaching at ECC for a couple of semesters and a fifth portion of one. The fifth-sized portion was my first crack at teaching in prison, and it was as a fill-in for a prof who'd been ejected for showing up (what the guards insisted was) fucked up. Her behavior getting out of and back into her car more than twice alerted them to watch her closely upon entry to the facility, wherein she was assessed to be hammered. She argued cold remedies; the prison didn't care what. They were happy to shuffle off a female professor in any case, no doubt more of a security challenge than they cared to manage in an all-male prison.

(At the time there was less overt ambiguity about who was male and who wasn't.)

So, after successfully taking over dopey's class for the last two meetings and the final examination, I was invited by the lovely titan Susan A_____, administrator of the academic wing, to return for a full course the following fall. I agreed because the money was good, her attitude was jubilant and encouraging, and no one asked me to be fingerprinted. That last part will matter in a minute, as will her lovely attitude.

Susan left for grander climes in the capitol the following spring, and a new admin was assigned, a male who was about 50, portly but thick in a football playing sort of way, and definitely not one to be enthusiastic about convicts going to college for free. Consequently, he didn't think much of these clown-ass professors coming in to make a few bucks teaching cons in classes his own colleagues could not afford to take on their shitty guard salaries.

He was not a happy man. Yet I could see his logic, little though it had to do with me, or so I thought.

He had the mind to be out a lot when I came to teach class, this term meeting in the chapel (where a man could pray or get a blowjob or both, according to one talkative client). So, in week 4 or 5, his staffer, a soft-spoken, kind lady but overly demurring, reminded me of my need to be fingerprinted. I told her I would not, by agreement when starting there the previous year. She said nothing but I heard a pencil scratching in her head.

The following week I was fully warmed up in class in the chapel, though as far as I could tell no one was yet praying or the other thing. We were talking about describing things by using familiar things to relate to the unfamiliar.

A gentleman was raising his hand to speak when the door opened. There stood a suit and a uniform, both filled by stern looking men in their 30's (a wee portly.) The suit raised his arm with that familiar authority and two fingers held at a 45 degree angle signed to me that I was to come with them.

"John Modaff?" he said, the melody of a command mixed with the syntax of a question.

"Yes," I said, noticing that my clientele was sitting back in the same way they would when someone was getting ready to hear a good story. Oh fuck. Did they find a roach in my car? Or bedbugs?

"Come with us. And bring your things."

A rustle went through the room that was barely vocal but had the same feel to it as when someone is about to get taken to the Principal's office.

"It's been great," I said to the boys, feeling that this had something to do with my missing fingerprints and that I would not be back.

I'd never been so glad to get out of prison as I was that day. When someone in a suit and someone in a uniform are both pissed, having been called away from their naps or electroshock therapy and not happy about it, getting to leave without an ass-jacking is a gift.

Glory to God.

Anyhow, I got back to campus and let them know what the suit told me: I was being ejected for refusing to be fingerprinted as was required of all facility staff.

NO way, I said. And, because this may have seemed boldly libertine and thus left wing as hell, my university superiors supported the revolution and said I did not need to feel obligated to go back if fingerprinting was a condition just now announced.

As I think it over now, I easily could have been forced back into finishing the course legally, as the university had a contract with the prison and I had one with the university. Still, a libertine mind was in those days an occasional target for respect, and the timing just happened to fall well for me.

I would lose the $1200 stipend but would gain the evident support of my Chair, Dean, and who knows whom. Done.

A few days later the Dean of Off Campus Programs, Dr. G__, called and asked if I would ride with him to the prison to discuss the class that had been interrupted. I said yes but that I had no intention of changing my mind concerning fingerprinting. With his assurance that he would not force that issue, we made plans to ride the following day to West L____ to meet with the warden.

On the drive over, which was about 20 miles through magnificent eastern Kentucky terrain, Dr. G had the wisdom not to ask me for an explanation, possibly figuring he'd hear one soon enough when the warden made inquiries.

The warden's office was the finest room in the prison, no surprise. It had none of the fluorescent harshness of the other offices, hallways, and rooms. Even the chapel was fluorescent. But Warden O___'s cave was special, rich in medium toned woods with dark highlights, chair rails, comfortable furniture that spoke of state-sanctioned power. Anything so nice in a state facility meant someone knew someone who knew where the money was. I was not aware at the moment, but the warden was a student at the University, getting his Master's degree. Perhaps that is why he exercised such patience with me.

We were not alone with warden O___. While he sat well lit at his desk, bathed in a yellow white pool of light from a brass desk lamp, lurking in the corner sat a woman whom I believe he introduced as counsel. This person could have crawled right out of Lewis' *That Hideous Strength*, smoking a cheroot and ready to use it to get information. She did not quite steam, but looked ready to be poked with a thermometer. Never said so, but her eyes and stiff slouch indicated a desire to fingerprint me from head to toe, if that could be done.

We got right to business after getting comfy. Pleasantries aside, the warden laid it out:

36

"This class has been paid for and we've got students who are matriculating on schedule. Canceling it now will create problems for all of them and for us. Can you see fit to complete the course if we can resolve the issues?"

"Yes," I said, "I did not wish to leave, but was asked to do so."

"For not agreeing to be fingerprinted at the behest of the academic coordinator?"

"That's what I was told. But I had also been told by Susan A____ when I started teaching here that I would not have to be fingerprinted. And I taught before without being fingerprinted. I would not have agreed to take this job if it was a requirement."

They all looked at me. Dean G___ with barely restrained glee, Warden O___ with a look one sees at zoos, and the cheroot tossing sideways glances that could cut meat.

"You will not be required to be fingerprinted if you agree to come back. That was a misunderstanding. Because you are not permanent staff, and spend so little time at the facility, we do not need for you to be fingerprinted. Is that agreeable?" Saying that last part seemed to hurt him, and I swear I heard the cheroot wince.

"That will be great. Status quo." I said. The Dean and I shuffled in a pre-departure sort of way.

"If you would," said the warden, as if placing a teacup, "could you tell us why you object to being fingerprinted?"

The question seemed sincere, and his shadowy pal in the corner stopped breathing to hear the answer.

"I'd be happy to. There are two reasons I do not wish to be fingerprinted. Malice and morons."

"Malice and morons?" the warden asked, as cheroot seemed to be searching for her gun.

"Malicious people can now create and place fingerprints using digital technology. The inherent corruptibility of digital fingerprint files makes malicious actions easier than ever. Simply switch one name with another. And this brings us to the morons."

The three of them waited as I framed it as delicately as possible.

"As unlikely as a malicious action may seem, particularly against someone as innocent and boring as me, it is very very likely that there will be errors made by morons who are careless, thoughtless, or just plain stupid. Every person who has fingerprints in the database is subject to such errors. Names will be placed with the wrong prints and vice versa. The only way to be free of malice and morons is to *not* have one's fingerprints in the system to begin with."

Feeling pretty sure I was the only person in the room who really gave any of that any credence, I stopped. Elaboration would be futile.

Clearly they'd all been fingerprinted.

"Well, that is an explanation," he said, glancing for the first time at his colleague, who seemed very disappointed at not getting to burn my chest with a lit match. "And thank you."

"Thank *you*," I said, a bit too cheerily, "I hated to lose the 1200 bucks."

That was crass; I can be without even trying sometimes.

Next episode: coming back to class....

But First: Getting Physical

Now a sleazeball might think this section is going to be about getting it on with students. Believe it or not, while there may have been opportunities, I rarely noticed them. True, the magnificent Kathy B __ did come into the office, which I shared with Mr. N__ at Hampton Institute, looking absolutely lovely and sitting down pertly with this announcement: "I've just come in to see your beautiful face." Mr. N nearly lost his teeth not noticing her from across the room, and I was momentarily speechless from exhilaration. She waited.

I said, "that's a nice thing to say," and changed the subject, hearing the words Mr. N had so often uttered replaying in my mind from other precarious occasions: "Watch your back." I'd have preferred to watch her back, but instead pretended to be interested in speech preparation tips or some shit. Fok.

Later that week, thinking that she might have been making a serious offer, I hauled my 23 year old ass over to the Campus Store, where Kathy worked. She was friendly but displayed none of the vivacity of her office visit. Had I dreamed what she said? I'll never know. From years past I suspect someone had made a bet with her that, sadly, she lost.

Another occasion of physical mention was on a the aforementioned student evaluation, wherein a student noted that I have an unpleasant feature, described as, "a huge forehead." It was either huge or large, I can't be sure. No one has ever mentioned my forehead, nor its size relative to the norm. So I was surprised by this observation and a little concerned. Had my forehead grown in the ocean air? The absence of decent mirrors in the house I was living in might have allowed this to happen without notice. I checked at a Phoebus shoe store, bending down to see my forehead in the shoe mirror. All was well, or the angle was favorable. In any case, that's the one time my forehead became top of mind, so to speak.

At Alfred University out in the boonies of Western New York, I taught classes in a miserable converted bus garage that had been carved up into offices and one constantly-used classroom. One day, surrounded by the lot of students in a horseshoe shaped arrangement, one of them said, "Why do you stand on an angle?"

"An angle?" I asked, suddenly aware of my attitude and my legs.

"Yes, you lean," she said. Several classmates nodded in friendly agreement.

"Yeah, why are you leaning?"

I first noticed they were correct, as I had been leaning slightly forward and to the right, as if standing against a gale. I straightened up, subtly but fully.

"You're right," I said, "I have been leaning. Huh!" And since then I've made an effort to stay on the level, even when urging forward against the cold, unforgiving, endless wind of sloth and apathy known as The Audience.

In Austin, teaching one of my first college classes for about a month, and fixing bicycles frequently on the side, I came to class wearing my usual unclean jeans. There were two reasons they were unclean: 1) I hadn't washed them, and/or 2) I had washed them, but insufficiently. This day some residue from bicycle chain sprockets had made a black fossil-like imprint on one of my thighs. A young man commented enthusiastically,

"You've often got the most interesting stains on your clothing."

I felt the compliment as it was intended, from one working stiff to another, and thanked him for noticing. We then proceeded to talk about communication or some shit.

LEAVE THIS SPACE BLANK. JUST BECAUSE

December 15, 2019

Been off here a while, wondering if writing about teaching makes any sense. The same question could be asked, though, about writing about anything. And, as Jane Francis once so profoundly noted, "If all activity is equally futile, why not have fun?"

And what is fun about teaching? Lots.

I can only speak for teaching college. I cannot imagine the horror of teaching children, whose parents would ever be in the wings, or worse yet in the room, judging whether little Duffy and Muffy were being treated not only well but equally well. God save us. This imbecility is creeping into the college classroom and onto the campuses, but more-so in those places where excesses of everything, including money and time, allow for it.

Fun.

No one ever said college ought to be fun, or that it works best when it is. My best classes were not fun, at least not in the normal meaning of the term.

Professor Whatonearth's course on Philosophy of Eastern Religions at SIU-C was not fun, but it was interesting, and mind-broadening, and mind-deadening at times. The teacher was a linebacker of knowledge, a balding caucasian who insisted on letting the sides of his topper grow out, in homage, perhaps, to the once Great Plains of his pate, now bereft even of fossils of hair.

The course was not fun during, nor was it funny. There was too much reading to do for that sort of thing. English translations of great verses of the past, the Upanishads, the Vedas, and all the rest too numerous and polyfluous to name today. Designata. The mess ran together into a summary that goes like this 40 years or more later: There is One. There is Other. And THAT is the problem.

Was the universe made to be carved up so? Why are dark and light adversaries rather than twins? Tis the boundary between the two that is most interesting, of course.

That class sticks with me 40 years later, as I vaguely know that there are Lots of Crazy Ideas all over the world, and many of them about God, and many of those far older than

Christianity and yet similar to it in certain principles, mainly as regards good behavior.

God love 'em! The chaps who sweep insects out of the way when they walk are striving for the same thing the penitent Catholic is: a world safe for bugs.

In classes of 300 or more I have learned as much as in classes with 15. Tis the teacher's doing in both cases, and mine. I recall Bob Trager, human giraffe, SIU Carbondale, 1977, teaching Introduction to Journalism (general education, forgive me), to a class of 350. He would lecture and display slides and lope about the room on two legs, grabbing leaves for snacking off of tall branches, freezing as if sensing a lion nearby if people would get to conversing in the remote rows. He'd freeze like that, waiting for the danger to clear, silent as a doe (or a giraffe), and then when things calmed down (and somehow they always did), he'd proceed, chewing and lecturing, until the forest was cleared.

Of the dozens and dozens of teachers I have had, tis difficult to choose one as The Best of All. Dr. Marvin Kleinau comes to mind, but for reasons other than perfectly sound teaching. He was motivating. That is every bit as important as being a fountain of minutiae. He cared enough to point out when I was being stupid, and noted on more than one special occasion that I could be quite the opposite when I tried.

He lives and we still correspond, though I was sad to see he thought retirement is for "for the dogs." Maybe he means he retired for the sake of the dogs who needed him. But I fear it means he was happier working. I am happy when busy, but working is a different thing. An artist is always busy, properly focused.

I am now five months from retirement
What started all of this? I know I am but a sliver of thread in the sport coat of education. But I am here now, and have been here since 1964 in one form or another. First as student, then as teacher, I've been breathing what breath I've had to breathe into the "system." Wrong metaphors. I've been dropping my bread crumbs on trails in five states. Some have picked them up. Some tread upon them. Others never noticed anyway.

But what started all of this? What started 56 years with at least one foot inside a classroom? I know why the years 1964 to 1987 happened: the first 12 were mandatory. And in the Modaff family, "you're going to college" wasn't a suggestion. I'm glad they insisted that it happen. Didn't take much of a nudge, though.

I knew I was going to try to be a teacher before I arrived in Carbondale. So, "it" started before that. There were so many teachers that I admired, many that I liked, and several that I loved (in more ways than agape.) Their job seemed fun. School, sadly, was the most interesting thing that ever happened to me. So the circus maximus was staffed by the learned ones, the dead serious, the flippant, the passionate (they always burned out because how could everyone else care as much?)--all of those types and more lit an incense of allure, an opportunity for wit, for performance, and to be admired, liked, even loved.

And dismissed. Always aware of being dismissed. The thing that saves the dismissive students in classes that I teach is that I understand them completely. Just let them be. Do not pursue. Lure.

Even a corpse can submit work if given enough of an extension.

Was the desire for me to teach the noble undertaking, preparing the leaders of tomorrow, etc? No. It was a show I knew I could play. It was a stage that felt like home. A stage in every way one can define that term.

I rode it out, since before I completed college, and enjoyed most of it, hated some of it, and detested just a few things. Not bad for a job. I've had other jobs where those proportions would shake out quite differently.

That brings to mind how teaching compares to other jobs. Which of my past occupations could be most aligned with teaching? Let's see. Mushroom farming, as with the raking of fresh manure and the aging of it to make a soil, a culture one might say? Or, bicycle repair, that simplest of mechanical pursuits, but a necessary one. Unlike automobile repair, nearly everyone is fully capable and intelligent enough to repair a bicycle. So it is with teaching. One just has to want to.

(Oh, and fuck not ending with a preposition here. Or anywhere.)

I almost killed a kid one winter morning while driving a school bus. Snowy morning, dusky light. I slid, he slid. Inches from disaster. That job was nothing like teaching. It was more important.

The best teachers along the way had very little in common. This showed me that students can take just about any style, as long as there is one.

How much is a person supposed to know to be known as sufficiently expert in a subject to "teach" it? Later on I will reflect on some odd practices in higher education that defy the idea that one ought to have had a class or two in a subject before trying to teach it.

Yeah, right.

Back to why. Some of the finest people I know, outside of family, have been my teachers. And the best teachers have treated my friends well. That shows style and solid nature. I try today to spy the various stages of relationship between students and stay out of the way. I've seen that happen since 1964, come to think.

Even some of the fucking nuns could do it--on a good day when their perpetual horniness and frustration did not spill into too exuberant renditions of the Stations of the Cross.

And, being as I am essentially a sloth in human form, there were features to teaching that seemed unique and worthy of desire. Freedom 4 months of the year, if one planned well and worked very hard the other 8. One would have to start one's own company, or get elected to Congress, to have that kind of time off with the blessing of the People. That's hard to miss, even for a kid.

And, I loved to read. That is nothing noble. I don't get all wet and creamy talking about reading. I think it is has fucked people up just as much or more than it has helped us. Still, when one loves to read, and to talk about reading, there is not really a more comfortable place than the classroom, now is there? OK, and a coffeehouse in the 19th century.

One can pretend, portend, purport, and resort to just about anything in the classroom. That leeway is an atrociously excessive grant given to teachers by a trusting community and nation. That leeway is pushed and prodded and squeezed from K through 12, and moving into 16-20 and beyond. Different than the 1960's, where the students rose up and insisted that the margins be blown open and topics in abundance should pour forth, today it is the professors, the children of the flower, and their children, who create courses, and thus define what is meant to be valuable knowledge.

Way too much leeway, and yet just the right amount. College is the last place that excess of just about anything is not just expected but is dearly paid for...

So back to why. There was going to be work no matter what I did. As lovely as the other jobs had been, shoveling, punching keys, and nippling spokes did not feel like endurable ways. And music? I'm pretty sure I'd hate making a job out of it. But I do like working in it at my leisure and 1 good song out of 100 ain't bad.

I play the guitar and sing at the start of each class because I believe anything can be interesting for 2 and a half minutes.

The wise have noted before us, 'tis more interesting than roll call.

Thus, dear reader, to know why I became a teacher, consider all of the above. Today, nearly 40 years since teaching Class #1, I enjoy the fading wisps of respect and conformity, wherein my excessive leeway operates, and give second chances and beyond in abundance. That used to mean something. Now students expect it, really. Being loose with standards is the norm.

50

Musings

Thousands upon thousands of students, inside the four walls, flowing like a river past my eyes (but a river that uses the door.) Some faces and names I remember. Some faces and speeches I remember.

I do feel this: teaching is dying. We will be replaced by Learning Machines. Tests* will prove that individuals can score above the norm learning by machine. The machine never gets tired. The machine behaves. The machine can be constantly updated as knowledge is developed and history is (re)written. The machine has access to all knowledge, all data, all literature, all music and art, all languages, all of time. The machine will crush teaching. Just a matter of when.

What will keep teachers and students in classes?

That somehow we do more than fatten our asses.

*scored by machine, no doubt

Jan 13, 2020

The day before the last first day.

Of course, short timers can index every day that way. I won't. OK, now and then. As Alli said today, "Today is the last last day of Christmas break." Dunnit.
This is the eve of the final first day, etc, then. A time of rarefied reflection, as a moment is unique in a way a photograph is: unmatched, but familiar enough to be of a species.

Reflection.

Isn't that teaching? How many new discoveries have been made while teaching, beyond pedagogical ones? One learns by teaching, the adage goes. But Rhetorick, an art as much as a science (as the chemistry of pigments is a part of art), demands mostly explanation, and the explaining of explaining.

Students will be challenged to stay awake as I lead them through the twiney ligaments of the corpus of my remaining knowledge. Having remembered many of the fragments I was able to grasp and hold along the way whilst a student, my general advantage now is seeing how they fit together. Has something been discovered, or have I just managed to arrange my tiles into what appears to be a picture of something?

Either way, it shall be delivered.

Two of the classes I will start again tomorrow did not exist in the imagination 20 years ago, and barely were conceived 10 ago. Social Media and Community. Ugh. May as well be Concussion and Intelligence.

They ARE related, you know.

OK, and

Conflict & Communication. Now there's a useful class. Students are naturally interested, with a few nudges and repetitions of activity, to look hard at their own most aggravating conflicts, and those of their friends and families. The major data are reports from students about what they live through and observe. We kiss the textbook's ass and learn vocabulary, but the main vein is out in the world, then brought in. This is one thing the classroom can offer that no other venue, as of yet, can do. People visibly empathize, sympathize, harmonize, clash, dismiss, and sleep through. All of it. Thank

you, Dr. William Sherman Minor. Thousands
of students have benefited from the curious
pause to look at communication, in a flavor and
with a melody you conceived. I have borrowed
so heavily from you, I simply cite you daily.

Why this apostrophe? Well, it is saying,
"this is what I would say if he were here or on
the phone."

Feelings about nearing the end of teaching
are a mixture of wondering how much I will
miss it along with I know what I WON'T miss.
The most astonishing change, I predict, will be
at last the dismissal of the School Year as an
organizing scheme for life. Since 1964 it has
been my calendar. Even when I was not in
school, my position was "between sessions."
It's goddamn 2020.

That's a long time to be at school, Mr.
Castorp.

Enough already. I have learned just as much
outside of school as in it, and much more of the
outside stuff has turned out to be practical.

There are moments I will miss. A classroom
suddenly lit up with a story, or a topic, or a
debate, or laughter, or dead silence that could
mean a dozen things. The occasional gesture of
appreciation, going both ways. The times when
I remember, as Nesbitt* says, to be the master
and so to let the student win. Let the student
win, but know along the way they will realize

you did so, at times, so they could learn to do that, too.

What I hated and will not miss. Grading. Not just because of the physically sapping positions necessary to handle the physical task of responding, but the idea that the output was a score, rather than an observation about state of mind and stage of practice. Look at all you have learned in your life NOT being graded and tell me grades are necessary for learning.

No, grading is something that schools have done to keep track of learning, and progress, that has been turned into a scoring system for Social Value. One must remember, friend, that only 1/3 of America saw fit to go to college at all...

And the other 2/3 work like dogs to help pay for it.

As for pay, however excessive my current salary may seem, it is more than balanced off by the decades I got paid squat for doing twice as much. What I was supposed to make happen, happened most of the time. And when it didn't, no one seemed to much notice.

*artist, teacher, veteran, and martial artist

What should have happened that did not? My 1000 radio commentaries cannot make up for having avoided the hot coals that must be tread to be published. Without brother Dan, and Robert H, I would not have any distinguished publications. With their help, there are but a few. Just enough. Those plus 1000 commentaries and all of the appropriate butt rubbing worked into a stew of Sufficiency. Alas, the days when my act, my actions, my style are appreciated and current, rhetorically quaint--those days are slipping away. This is not an illusion I've manufactured in order to justify hopping off the coach. Tis among the several reasons to go.

Who deserves credit for my radio commentaries? Just opinions. But somehow adequately engaging to be continued, through a dozen Overseers at the radio station. When will I no longer fit there? But whom to thank:

Mom, for diction and articulation guidance, with firmness.

Marvin Kleinau, who reminded me that people have dreams and some live on dirt roads.

William Minor, or rather, Bill. For that ballet of provisionalism without permissivism's excess.

All of the Oral Interp teachers: Lynn C. Miller, Paul Gray, Marion Kleinau (Marvin's boss), Jim Van Oosting, Eric Petersen, Kristin Langillier, and out of class Bob Modaff. How to love a script without slobbering on it was part of what they taught.

How I got off here on radio commenting is unknown, except it does relate to what helped me create the illusion of being a professor, an act so refined I could once even begin to believe it was true. But it wasn't. As my pal Oscar the anarchist goatherd once mused, I was an outsider on the inside. I got this blue collar turned inside out and managed to get up near the tall grass, the thin air, or is it the deep water? Choose your medium, I played along and got along. There were even moments where the fact that I was the one sitting or standing there made a difference to how things went, and they went well. That was not, of course, always the case.

For all of those latter moments I duly apologize. One should leave one's attitude on the porch.

...this last semester, this last "term," will be one where the flavor is savored. I need to remember, and act knowing this, that asking questions is much more useful than making speeches.

February 12, 2020
4 months out

At the start of class, I close the door as close to the hour as possible, maybe 30 sec early. Grab up the guitar and sit down in the chair, placed there when the room was arranged about 15 minutes before the main mob breezes in... for years, there was a new quote each day, written in chalk and then when that disappeared, written in "erasable marker." Somehow this made chalk seem quaint and old school, which I guess it was but it was also normal. Blackboards were black when they were invented, green later on, but still called blackboards or just boards. Now everything's a

58

white board. More conspiracy? Whiteboard supremacy?

Often after the song I take lately to asking if anyone has anything they need to get off their chest. Today a student asked, "are you getting a little sad that you are retiring?" I said, a bit quicker than I would have rhetorically chosen to, or had hoped would be natural, "Yes." But of course, an accurate answer, for which there was no time, was that only some things will be missed, but the most of it won't, including having to try twice as hard to play even the same old chords, much less new ones. And as this has become harder, this has become more of a job, and that's just not right for someone seeking to avoid work.

Every now and then just the right question gets a hand up that's never been up and a voice spoken on purpose and with purpose that has not spoken thusly. That is a sign, I have claimed since 1980, that something good is going on. Even if the person spurts nonsense, they're spurting*. It's a start.

*I'm really surprised "spurt" is not getting underlined in red by Word. Huh.

Random thoughts.

Rather than dreading retirement due to the aforementioned Encounter With Nothingness, aka Freedom, I merely dread wondering if I will dread it. The filtered rose-colored glasses will

screen out the folly and aggravation of
pretending to be a professor, and the remaining
memories might add up to something I miss, but
not really something I ever had. Gotta
remember that.

There was romance in being the professor
before I became one. The most horrifying thing
is how many classes I have taught that I didn't
have a shred of special work in preparation. Not
that uncommon, according to legend. So, what
are students paying for again? A fast reader
who knows how to devise evocative questions?
Robots will soon be doing that, if they aren't
already.

The romance was in being the student,
seeing the professor, listening, watching the life,
the implication of tremendous freedom, and also
the millstone of academic politics--but that last
was always an aside to the students. We saw
what the profs intended us to see, and little
more. The best they had, we got. Our best?
They caught a whiff of it now and then.
Lopsided. But we were, after all, the clients.

Being, or pretending to be, a professor for so
many years, qualifies me to say what one could
be: not an impostor, not a fraud, just about
regular. Average. Common in the sense of well
dispersed and plentiful. And thus my vantage
is, perhaps, one commonly held, shared even,
among many professors who size up their actual

knowledge comparing it to what they could or should know.

A pea versus the sun.

As the sap running from a bear has only to be faster than the friend who is also running, the professor can be just that far ahead, and bear the torch, as it were, even though one's actual knowledge is about 15 pages and a week ahead of the fastest student in the room. Not a word, said Mynheer Peeperkorn!

"Can you read? You're teaching this..." a textbook is proffered by a Chair. Actually happened 3 days out from starting at Hampton Institute (now University), though the boss didn't say "can I read." You begin a new subject, days away from the start of the term. This is how money is made and footnotes endured.

I may have mentioned it before but I think I might miss my building and office and room keys the most. Having keys to a 15 million dollar building is nice harbor in a storm or when one has to pee on a stroll. Then again, I never ought have been let in there without constant adult supervision.

======= *world changes forever*=======

March 21, 2020

Since I last sat here to write about teaching, the world has changed. I know that would be true no matter when or where I was writing, but this is different. This is huge. This is looking like the biggest mess we've ever been in, partly due to nature, mostly due to human nature, and perhaps worst of all due to American human nature.

My plan for ending college teaching was to go out as spring ended and summer began, trees leaving while the students packed to do the same. Casual, unhurried goodbyes to those students and colleagues who have noticed and been noticed by me. All of that pettifogical indulgence is gone, now, because of two tragedies:

1) the emergence of a new virus that appears to have originated in China in late 2019. In the order of prior Chinese viruses, like MERS, and SARS and others, this virus is possibly ten times worse than seasonal flu in morbidity and mortality. Coronavirus, aka COVID-19, was not contained. It spread without significant barriers for weeks. On a small world where 2 million people are in the sky going somewhere else each and every day, not much time is needed to spread something like this.

2) the reaction to the virus in the United States. For a host of reasons perhaps too mundane or obvious to get into here and now, America has reacted what appears to be too drastically in some respects, and not quickly or drastically enough in others. Therefore, as usual, the waiting until the controllable phases have passed means the actions necessary are ever more drastic.

And they are.

Entire states are telling people to stay in their homes, to "shelter in place"--a warning formerly presented to victims of natural disasters such as storms and manmade mayhem such as chemical leaks. California is essentially closed for business. New York, too. People are telecommuting wherever possible, but we all know that the real work, the real production, the making of things, growing of things, transportation of things, relies on people being together in common effort. This cannot happen when we are told to keep 6 feet apart and stay home, only to venture out for food, medicine, or emergencies. I fear that, soon, simply to get food and medicine will themselves be emergencies. We stock up but how much can be kept?

But why do I write of this mayhem here, in this pleasant perlocution about my quiet life as a teacher? Because these two things ended my time teaching abruptly, without fanfare or poetic swan songs. Nobbut. I feel ashamed for writing about what I have lost, knowing that already people have lost so much and right now hundreds of thousands are losing their jobs.

I know I will soon be retired, but also wonder how a system that cannot work can continue to provide payments... And the solution, to go to work, would not be possible in any case.

And yet, there was a glimmer or two at the end of classroom teaching on March 11. A few students, including a couple of whom I'd barely imagined appreciated my strange freak show, expressed in ways that could not and did not involve touching, that they were touched by the experience in class. As one said, when I announced they would no longer be inconvenienced by having to come to class, "That does not mean we won't miss it." A nice thing to hear. Another put it this way, "you've been a good teacher. All the other ones suck." As sideways as that compliment is, one is pleased not to suck.

I write today aware that you, dear reader, will likely be reflecting on the words of one who is gone. Soon or late, when have we ever known when the end is to come? People die at every age. Who expects it? A fraction of a percent? To everyone else, despite evidence to the contrary, death comes as a surprise.

What has that got to do with teaching? Perhaps just this, that the influence of a teacher having taught well or inspired, breaks free of that teacher like a shell of a bug, and provides what it can with no need of the teacher forthwith and forever. And if there is succor in the living reflection that one might have made a difference, then this now is me enjoying that liberty.

The subject my very last day addressing a class normally assembled in The World Before the Mayhem Began was a disturbance in the social network of his day, as Thomas Paine released his *Common Sense*. I read a few portions, but was driven by the subject of the course (Social Media and Community), to explain how what he said and how he said it blended with the means to say it widely and an audience that was hungry. All of this cobbled up into a rush of support for revolution.

All it takes is the intense pressure of oppressive government plus time to make the diamond of rebellion shine. All governments need to know that, but particularly, said Paine, the government of and by kings.

I did not say this in class, but it occurs now that there has emerged--thanks to social media and The People knowing themselves and becoming aware (as the ancients feared) that they could vote their own comfort--there has emerged a new Monarchy: the People as King. Representatives, in constant fear of dismissal or worse, fawn and flee toward accommodation and the obvious or signaled reduction of pain. At all costs the representatives now strive to please the People, who can crush them with social media in a flash. And the People, of course, as people do, wish and demand when they can that they be made as comfortable as possible. In this the People are as children, because they are not aware that they are capable of asking the host for something that will destroy the host. Children do not understand why, if their parents have money, the parents will not spend it for the immediate comfort of the child. The People are this way today. And the saddest part is that they are asking the government for help when it is the same government that is, in the name of protecting the People, harming them and causing the employment and debt crises and all of the attendant problems.

Which brings us back to the pin that pricked this bubble: the virus.

To do the right thing to control it is to do the wrong thing for liberty. This is the exchange. If I want to avoid drowning, I must climb into a crowded, uncomfortable, dangerous, rocking lifeboat. This is the bargain. This is where we are.

Trying to get back to writing about teaching:

The impact this is having on schools, colleges, and universities will change the landscape of education like a volcano, earthquake, and fire all at once. For months BEFORE COVID reports had averred schools were on the edge, with private schools closing by the dozens and public schools fighting harder for a shrinking pie (even as spending goes up.) Schools will close, articles said. Soon.

For now, colleges like Morehead State have chosen to make the bulk of the education they provide an "online education." This is a helpful short term plan, but risks exposing a truth about education: students CAN do most of it on their own. Or, the students who can do it mostly on their own are the ones who need college even less than others.

Yes, there is the social, cultural, view-expanding nature of college life, of campus culture. But is that what people have been paying $25K a term for? Maybe not.

So MSU and other schools are now "online" for the most part. I have been conducting certain classes online for 20 years, so this is no shock. But many institutions are moving from classroom to internet in the span of 5 or 6 days, during a time they planned to "break" from teaching, and are now "pivoting" into a "delivery method" that is alien to many teachers, their students, and thus to teaching and learning. All that aside, the revelation that this can be done at all, even poorly, has got have people wondering about the wisdom of ever going back to a campus.

I predict here and now, March 21, 2020, a MASSIVE increase in enrollments for established, reputable online universities that already have their shit together. Students are going to say, "if I'm going to go to college online, why not go to an online college?"

The clatter in the Ivy draped buildings will be window blinds slapping broken glass. Or not.

Maybe this crisis will come and go more quickly, due to the stringent measures being taken. And while the economic harm already done, plus what is coming, will reverberate longer than the root cause, we may be able to get together safely once again, or rather, more safely than today.

Meantime, my classroom career in teaching ended March 11, 2020. What is lost? Less than the fart of a mosquito in a hurricane. But oh, it was a splendid flatulation.

Is this simply more pedantry? If so, my apologies. If not, go hug a teacher, if it can safely be done.

June 12, 2020

The virus and now the riots and protests
not too loosely related have stolen, for a while,
the urge to write, to play, to sing, to compose.
In this way all of it encourages decomposition.
The risk of enduring events that can obscure
nearly all other features of life, or threaten to
alter them, is that memories which might have
easily or readily been recalled fall into disuse, or
worse yet, obscurity borne of an illusionary
insignificance. "Why write about my first day
of _______ while the world is on fire?" Why,
indeed. More important than ever since, if the
end is nigh, a quick gathering of reflections

might be all that is left to us when experience finally erases the details that even now grow faint, like a painting fogged over by the soot and grime of decades of hands and breath.

My first day of school (1st grade) was my first day of teaching, as the latter grew out from the former, and each school day either taught me something to do or something not to do as a teacher. Mostly what not to do.

Even now it seems petty to be writing when I could be mounting an impassioned defense of liberty or kumquats or something.

Details:

St. Joan of Arc Catholic School, Lisle, IL. First grade. 1964. Nuns everywhere. I'd seen them before but never this many in one place. And not a priest among them. The strongest visual memory is entering the classroom and being led by Sister Miriam to my desk, next to Paul Wagner whose name, like mine, had been printed on a card that was taped neatly to the upper right corner of the desktop.

I would find out later that sisters had a thing for the upper right corner.

As I recall, Paul was normal looking with all the right parts in the right places, and he wore glasses, which at the time seemed cool. Glasses suck except for the frontal eye protection provided against most things short of a bullet. Oh, and seeing.

I don't remember much else about first grade, except there was a lot of paper folding, and sister's hands were such a blend of soft yet worn that when she folded the yellow, lined paper into vertical columns for keeping things straight when we printed, the sound was a creakly crunch of softness not to be imitated elsewhere in life.

That may have been sister Cecilia in 3rd grade or some time, but one old nun is, for the most part, built the same as other nuns, save for Sister Charlotte Eileen, who stood out in several ways that must be considered as school became the locus of sex (potential, kinetic, actual) for the next, say, ever.

But first grade also offered insights into the vomitus of other children, which itself led to the discovery that cleaning up vomitus is a "privilege." I'd never heard that word before, as in my now observably parental homeplace egalitarianism meant there was no occasion to use the word. Privilege almost always included going beyond the routine. One could be allowed to stand outside the door and wait for a guest, or run to the office with a message or for the new box of pens (pens!) Or haul milk, or hot dog bags on Hot Dog Day, or, as it was in the early grades, *anything*, including sweeping up the puke-soak compound (really just a greenish kitty litter), dumping it, and taking the bin where it needed to be. The honor! To be trusted with the mixture of vomitus and green vomitus-soaking compound, broom, and dustpan. Indescribable. I am not sure if I got to do it more than once, but it meant so much.

In addition to vomitus, the contrast of teachers was a first lesson. Sister Miriam, as I recall a portly, jolly, clean-shaven nun, my very first teacher (I never went to preschool), fell ill halfway through the year and was replaced by another nun whose name has barely been forgotten. As I recall Sister 2 was thinner and not quite so nice, and may have been the one who turned me in for stuffing unfinished papers into my desk. The horror! While I liked a lot of teachers through the years, I trusted very few of them after that episode.

The alphabet printed in caps and lower case, white writing on green cards, a globe, the heaters, oddly placed 'neath the windows, and the windows, the most glorious part of the room, the place that reminded one the world still existed despite the crushing routines and demands of elementary school. One learned discipline in a room with windows, for they ever called the eye and often the ear, while teachers and burdens placed by them demanded Attention to the Task At Hand. Clouds demanded nothing, but were much more adorable than the bloodied Jesus hanging in front, center, on the wall, crucified, above the chalkboard and underneath the clock.

Fragment: a sister explaining to us that the crucifix we stared at in room after room was probably not accurate, and that the spikes driven through the palms of the ceramic Jesus would more accurately be placed through his wrists. He would need to be able to pull himself up to breathe, she went on, savoring the correction of history and giving us some insight into Roman executions.

Ahhh, elementary school.

But let's not get too diverted from the Catholic things. Even though the first 5 years were steeped a dark brown by the tea of religious discipline delivered by a range of nuns only lightly salted by "lay persons"--the nuns had nearly disappeared from the faculty by 8th grade, with one remaining like a face on Mt. Rushmore.

Sister Alberta.

Perhaps she has been quoted prior but here's a dutiful repetition:

"You get yourself a reputation, you have to pay the consequences."

Inspirational.

Yet her near constant smirk seemed to reveal that she knew we knew the whole thing was a show and that while she was dead serious about her God and her religious habit(s), our situation as to eternity did not keep her up at night.

Second grade: Miss McShane, a kind and somewhat farmish young teacher who loved horses.

Third grade: Sister Cecelia, thin as a shadow, skin like crepe. Quiet. If you wanted to hear her, and thus to survive, or to earn "merits" you had to be quiet, too. In third grade I fell in love with Cathy Harris. We traded pictures. I went to her house some years later and she looked at me confirming she did not remember things like I did.

That's how memories are. We have them but we're probably the only ones that do, as for most of them. So, while recalling and recording may seem trite, there is no other way. When sister Alberta's sub, Ms Gertrude L___, heard someone bragging (possibly me) she announced to the whole class that "self talk stinks," and should be avoided and unrewarded.

She had a point, but to stop would kill all of biography and first person narration.

June 24, 2020

Amidst the growing pandemic of coronavirus that started in China at the end of 2019, protests against imaginary "systems" that are invoked to deflect individual culpability or standing, amidst spending like the world has never seen by governments that are confiscating more from the people than ever before, amidst economic collapse inspired greatly by the former, amidst logically foreseen and predicted threats of even greater maladies to come, I take some more time to write about teaching.

Why not?

As Jane Francis once said, "Compose or decompose."

Going grade by grade in detail would be onerous and imbalanced, as some years stand out, or some events stand out, that cement each differently.

Fourth grade we, the combined malcontents, already jaded without knowing the word, were so evil one day we made Miss Michelle McShane sit at her desk and cry hot salty tears. That sprouted my first tendril of realization that teachers might be people too.

Fifth grade, I got a mad crush on Charlotte Eileen. I had begun to notice the shape of things, not just faces and voices, and she had just the right everything, to my 5th grade mind. Though I am sure I wouldn't have had the slightest idea of what to do with her if she'd let me touch her. But that wasn't the main problem, as I had pledged my interest before to a girl or two. Charlotte Eileen's first name was "Sister."

Yes. She was a nun, of the Benedictine Order. Or OSB, as I recall. You figure it out.

Her being a nun, but young, vivacious, and beautiful in every way did not help. Nuns were supposed to be hideous mongers of terror and deference, to them, to The Lord. Charlotte Eileen was none of that. She defied everything, but dammit she was a nun.

Sex with nuns? "None." It's the root of the word. Anyway, I was years away from fucking a teacher. She did engage lively conversations, bring music into the classroom, occasionally allow a rare disdain for the Cathlick way, and smile when the crusty old nuns who visited with hairy eyeballs left the room.

She would attempt to firmly discipline us, but could be broken into happiness. Her command to the entire class to make 100 paper airplanes as punishment for wasting time making paper airplanes could have been logically refuted if we'd thought it over. But we were compliant, because the punishment could never be as bad as Geography.

So we began to fold, realizing each of us had to make only 4 to be done in minutes. Thinking practically, which meant thinking about how to slow things down, we assembled unionized work groups with strict subtextual orders to arrange production to be slowed. CE left the room and we quickly finished, waiting for her return. When she came, a tsunami of paper airplanes headed in her direction at the doorway, and for a moment the blackness of her habit was eclipsed by our foldings. She smiled, and ordered us to clean up.

We did not get out of Geography.

Like an idiot, which I was quite a lot and perhaps still am, I pined terribly for Charlotte Eileen all that summer of 1969. My summer of lost love. Moping, wasting away, barely living. Rotten with juvenile angst. For a nun. I took to watching for a car that might be hers, or someone walking. A friend had a picture that included her in the frame, walking away, half out of the shot, head turning over her right shoulder, the crisp white of her collar defining her neck, and the loose, wild hair that showed under her perfect bride of Jesus coif.

Why should this be shared in my pack of lies about Teaching? Because since Day 1, my teachers made lots of impressions but one of them stood out: "that wouldn't be a bad way to make a living." She seemed happy.

We might blame decent and indecent teachers for a lot of the fools that are teaching today. Inspiration, doled out like lather, can be a dangerous thing.

Seventh grade, Mrs. Louise Collins, who tempted us to research "goofy" in the dictionary, was short and all business, taught us bo-koos about Mythology. Yes, lots of learning of stupid names and stories, historically trending even these millennia later (huh! before the internet, too). Makes for a good time during *Jeopardy* now. Less valuable during *Wheel of Fortune.*

Seventh grade was also a dose full of Sister Alberta, the aforementioned Holy Terror With A Smirk. And there was Dr. Mukherjee, science teacher with a PhD, who had such a contagious accent that we could not help but make fun while also working to refine our impersonations. She loathed "story books" but said the phrase "sto-lee-booooks--I will tolerate no sto-lee booooks in my class." If I recall correctly, a rumor circulated that Jim Kelly and associates deliberately brought in library books with stories about India. She is most famous among her progeny not for teaching scientific method well enough, but for having a poster on the wall, stating "You are what you Eat." When she read it aloud, she added to it, "When you it biff you arl biff." She replaced "ee" with the short "i" routinely, so you get the result, wot? She ate no biff.

God bless her sweet Hindi soul.

Mrs. Leitel was famous in 7th and 8th grade for having the saggiest tits anyone had ever seen up close (covered, of course.) She did a better job of teaching science because, I'm sorry, someone wearing veils is harder to take seriously. Mrs. Leitel would have looked better in Dr. M's clothes, though.

As for tits, boys notice them, in case you hadn't heard. Part nature, part nurture. Sure The Culture accents the breast in many places, but we did not need any prompting to find them interesting. Still don't. The whole Free The Nipple movement might have done a lot of good in removing the distraction that covering always causes. Many years were to pass before any one of us could comprehend what life had to do to a person to have tits as saggy as Mrs. Leitel's.

Eighth grade, Mr. Mack ("My name is Mackarowski. You can call me Mr. Mack not mack, not John, but Mr. Mack or Mr. Mackarowski.") And, his most tenacious punishment, "Write the glossary." This to anyone who dared to cross the line, which was a line between when a walrus wakes up and snorts or decides to continue its nap.

George Essig: who continued the trend started by Sister Charlotte Eileen and dragged popular music into the classroom for "appreciation and analysis." I guess he figured we wouldn't read stories or watch films. Anyways, he brought in The Moody Blues (whose lyrics now appear to vary from enlightened to inane), Jesus Christ Superstar (which I thought was ballsy as hell given the place being Cathlick.)
I just need to comment right here that WORD didn't recognize "coronavirus" but did recognize "ballsy." Just sayin'.

George Essig did get red faced mad as hell, long before Howard from *Network*. Someone appeared to have stolen someone else's lunch sack from the high shelf above the coat hooks. The horror! For effect, he plunged a set of essays we'd written on ethics or some shit into the trash to amplify his rage. It was somewhat less convincing when the folks in 8A later heard him doing precisely the same speech in 8B. Lesson learned: Rage, when rehearsed, loses rhetorical heft.

St. Joan of Arc was perhaps a heroic place. The buildings ranged from nearly ancient (early 20th C.), as in the original church, to sparkly and new, as in the Junior High which linked to the new church and gym. Near the end of the 70's a magnificent million dollar church was built that looked like a cynic's case of the shits, but I was gone by then. The beloved old church had a scary, creepy, guilt- and lust-laden appeal, and the swipes at grandeur and wasting money given by the bereft that tinged it with the Glory of Rome. The new church looked like a stall.

I often dreamt of being in the old church, wandering through many nonexistent doors into truly glorious, opulent, profanely rich rooms, Property of the Pope, I suppose.

There was a school section on the second floor of the old church, where our wee parents went to school. There was a basement where dances and "smokers" were held, names given to the usual chances at getting some. There was a goddamn BAR in the basement, forchrissakes. I shit thee not (Romans).

And then there was the third floor, which could be exited in two ways, down the stairs that brought you up or through the black metal pipe that provided a fire slide as an escape. Of course we loved to try to climb all the way up the slide, but the dark was really dark up there and besides, at the end was a door; that door led to the apartment of one Mrs. Brogel Anyhow, she was as old and fat as the building, with skin the color of a sodden bar towel. She smoked, looked with eyes that had seen it all and were willing to dump it all on your ass, and clearly gave not a fuck. And she was scary to kids, though she probably loved them. Who else could stand to eat one every day for breakfast?

My last hug on the place was becoming groundskeeper in the summer of who knows what, clipping around buildings (by hand, in the days before weed whackers) hauling debris here and there, trimming hedges, scraping gutters, breaking every rule OSHA had yet to invent. Falling asleep on the old FarmAll tractor with the grass cutter spinning below, on a hill, near the ditch. Good times.

I thought I might become a priest once for about 5 minutes. I was walking home from "altar boy" duties one Christmas break, having chosen to do the duty for a string of days. Maybe they were paying, who knows. But walking home, out the church steps to the walk, the street, the snow falling, the air still, a peaceful feeling that I later learned was the fruit of habit met up with proximity to the St Joan of Arc, and I nearly got "called." This "calling" people talk of even now is really the confluence of a bunch of things that don't have much to do with one another. Still, I can sympathize and understand how someone might get inspired and end up becoming clergy.

Thank God I had Christmas to take my mind off of becoming a priest that year.

I graduated the 8th grade in 1972. I remember tearing ass home on my bicycle, unable to get away from that place fast enough. And even today, though one is tempted, I cannot say that those were good old days. Most of them were spent in anguish, or boredom, or fear, with lots of guilt (some of it deserved, much cultivated). Being boxed in by church, school and parental surveillance was just too much. The ride home took a minute or less that evening.

Although this is a missive on Teaching, remembering the incidents and places and people of "learning" must be relevant. I did steal something from every decent teacher I ever had, and probably several things from the shitty ones, too.

"You get yourself a reputation, you have to pay the consequences."

Smirk.

June 25, 2020

Once again overcoming the urge to nap and thus to forget for a while the looming clouds of chaos and destruction, which I hope are just figments of my imagination, as they have always been. Trouble is, now everyone else is talking about them, too. Shit. But they've all been wrong before, say, like about Michael Jackson. Though he wasn't contagious in quite the same way that fear and viruses can be.

In my loose chronology, I am finishing up my teacher training at the elementary level by graduating from St Joan of Arc, which Fr. Jude the Dude used to call Joan By Arc, which I heard as Joan by Ark, which didn't make a lot of sense but was a grand image: her standing there in the forming winds, thin but armored quite ahead of her time, sword drawn, daring any of the pairs of creatures to fuck around on the gangplanks.

So I left St Joan by Ark in 1972. That summer is a blur. High school began, and maybe someday I will tell all about what happened there but 90% of it is so predictable that you'd probably want to hang yourself if I started details. So, once again, hopping from teacher to teacher and memorable moment to moment, I recall how high school helped me become a teacher, or rather, to continue to want to become one.

In grade school the authority of teachers came from the church, from *in loco parentis*, and from God His Holy Self, since he ran the church and the church ran the school. In public high school, the authority of teachers came as much from consenting parents as it did from The State (a titan too large to see at the time.) Teachers' reputations emerged mostly from their own histrionics. Some notorious teachers were feared prior to the first day of class, and one of them was Mr. Clarence Jensen.

I was scared shitless of Clarence Jensen. He looked like Einstein having a good hair day, but had none of AE's bicycle-riding charm. Jensen was known for cruelty, gnawing off limbs, eating freshman whole, and sending people to the Office for a permission slip to be let past the locked door if they arrived late. Since his Science classes were downstairs, about as far as away from the Office as you could be without leaving the building, a trip there and back could eat up another 15 minutes of class time so it was a strange mix of punishment and vacation. Like the Klinghoffer's vacation.

My first time in Jensen's class I had been primed for maximum fear by brother Ken, his pal Chuck Knight, and siblings Mary and Bob. Horrible. Out of control. Unstoppable. And these were their compliments.

Mr. Jensen's demonstrations of his cattle prod and hand-cranked electric generator convinced everyone that falling asleep would best be avoided. The consequences for being late were as promised, but I never saw him eat anyone, limb or whole.

I had him again when I was a sophomore and either on a test or some sort of information card I wrote, "I used to be scared of you but I'm not anymore." He stopped near my table, handing back or picking up whatever and said, "what is this, true confessions?" But the glint in his eye, which really always was there but I'd missed it looking for tentacles, glimmered a bit brighter that day.

Thus I learned from him that being tough in policy didn't mean being a complete ass in practice.

Alan Munneke: PhD English literature teacher, or should I say professor. Having a professor in high school meant independent work, self-pacing, and lots of sarcasm. He had boxes of shit we had to work through while he read who knows what at his desk and answered occasional questions. He would have us read our own stuff out loud, or read it aloud himself to give us the rare thrill of having a competent reader utter our own writing. Sometimes he lost it and his eyes rolled up into his head so far he could study his own thoughts. Other times he lost it in hilarity, as when my brother Bob ended an essay on family life with a parody of *The Waltons*: "Good night Mary Jo. Good night Margaret. Good night Billy. Fuck you, Grandpa." Or something like that. But Big Al read every word of it and nearly cried with joy. He should have been fired, I suppose, for saying "fuck," but it was the 70's and no one gave a.

John Mulcare, friend of the family and dear to my own mother, was another Phd, teaching Chemistry. I knew better than to take a class from him but found his facial antics so amusing I stored them away as a repertoire to use myself when teaching and seeking to fight the cold stares of existential crisis coming from the rows.

Beverly Fiore, speech and drama and cinema teacher, taught me that a voice can be liquid, that love of a subject means you don't need notes, that giving student lots of rope can be fun either way, whether they end up hung or not, and that a teacher's job is a 7 day a week project. She was a dynamo and very patient while also being out of her mind with energy.

There are other teachers who influenced me in high school, but mainly in what NOT to do. Learning by example also works very well when the example is a negative.

I met one of the loveliest teachers I've ever known in high school, but the details of that relationship will have to be told elsewhere or never. Let's just say that there are things one cannot learn in the classroom that can go quite well elsewhere. Not being coy, but sharing details right now feels inappropriate, and as that is a feeling I almost never have, I am noticing it and responding by moving on. What did I learn from her that helped me as a teacher? How easily things can happen, and what to watch for...

June 29, 2020   *Teaching As/And Theater (or Theatre)*

Teaching is a performance, as the cliche goes. What that worn out aversion leads to is a sense of fakery or putting on, which both might be true, especially on days when one would rather be sleeping. But performance is theatre, and theatre is the conversion of text and script into sound and movement, and this teachers do all of the time. We convert texts into something palatable, if we are doing our jobs. This is most challenging in math and other abstractions with unbending practical results. In the humanities our task is much easier, for our theatre is the theatre of poetry and play and music. We've got it made as far as basic material goes. After all, what is the mathematical equivalent of Bukowski?

To take the dry stuff of fact, evidence, and theory or to teach the tools of detailing sound and movement, and to make it conceivable, valuable, and practical by showing and singing--this is the theatre of teaching in humanities.

There is a science of speech, the clinical side, the linguists bickering over narrow transcriptions, of anatomy and therapy--playing with those folks can be as bad as math class, though they are every bit as necessary. The other side of speech teaching is the performance side, the art side, the rhetorical side. And there was no better place to study that than UT and SIU. I was lucky. Most everyone was still thrilled at the prospect of another show (class), though a few were near enough the end of their careers that their fatigue was beginning to show, as I am sure mine did some days in my last years.

From the above one sees, then, the value of the song at the start of the class. Not quite the national anthem, but paradigmatically kin to it. And certainly in the place of the "overture" one would expect with any decent story about to be performed.

The speech teacher has to make articulatory phonetics as captivating as the Rhetoric of ______. Who memorializes Dwight Bolinger in the way he deserves? No one but a few geeks. He invented the term "speech melody" as far as I'm concerned.

The current crisis with the coronavirus pandemic has led to lots of nonsense about the value of wearing masks. The experts trotted out to speak in rational ways on behalf of the President also had to lie to people in order to prevent insane runs on equipment that "front line health workers" needed. They needed masks, etc b/c they are known to reduce the risk of infection and contraction by patients and medical staff. The lying meant that for a while people went about without masks. But now, oh my! the train has been turned, and someone has to unload all of these crazy masks, oh AND now the same experts who a month ago said no need to wear a mask are saying everyone should wear one nearly all of the time. I am bringing all of this to mind to get to a point about what is going to happen to the Theatre of Teaching, particularly to the teaching of speech appreciation and performance. Black out the bottom half of your face. Everything is suddenly radio.

That might not be a problem for some, but most people aren't suited to be interesting with their entire face, much less the top half of it. Granted, the focus shifting to the eyes is proving that a lot of ugly people have really beautiful eyes. For them the masks are an improvement, making all of our lives better medically and aesthetically. But for people trying to express the subtle flavors of sarcasm, wit, teasing, irony, humor, punning, and authenticity--we're doomed.

Once again, or rather, for yet another reason, I am very glad I stopped trying to teach when I did. I cannot miss It, for the It that was there when I was there is gone--way beyond merely "not being able to go home any more." This home has burned down, as long as the masks are on the faces. Everything that can be expressed, taught, and learned from the nose down to the neck is lost to us now.

Oh fok it I'm glad I don't have to do radio and make eyes in classrooms or worse yet over the web. Soon enough people will realize that teaching machines are superior in online and remote instruction and professors will be replaced by avatars in possession of the entirety of human knowledge -- and "who" never get tired.

College teachers taught me a lot about teaching too. Then next time I sit down here I shall run through the highlights. The main vein is that I entered college convinced I'd prepare to teach high school (good God!) but was soon convinced by the silted, stuffy, lapidary nonsense of Education about Education that I had to make a break. Where could one teach without lesson plans? College! And the people were cool...

Dr. Roderick Gordon, teaching "Acoustics of Music" for some reason as a general education course, engaged me and 300 others in Lawson Hall, invited fascinating speakers, gave worthy demonstrations, and made the most out of the overhead projector--and all of this while quite often either drunk or having strong effects of having been. How might one expect to even be noticed by such a man, in a room so overflowing with faces that all looked the same? And yet, one day when I happened to cross paths with him on the square in front of Shryock Auditorium, he perked up and said, "Hello, H-8!" And kept jaunting.

H-8 was my seat number.

Huh.

Oh, his TA was adorable, worked doing all the shitty stuff, and got me in the habit of checking on who was who in big classes. SIU-Carbondale was the one place I had huge classes like that. Vestiges of the Golden Age. A bodhi tree so large 300 could sit beneath it and have room for a projector and a screen. I've always thought I could put on quite a show in such a setting, and never had the chance to dance before more than 60 or so at a time in regular classes. OH well. There's always the internet.

July 2, 2020

Started this reflection a year ago or so, as usual not even imagining what could or would become of the world. There is much to say about Things In General, but as the purpose of this is to reflect on teaching (and therefore studenting), general concerns will have to be alluded to along the way. Suffice it for now to say that it looks like we're headed for the Second Great Depression. This might better be called The Big One, since we're all gonna get fucked except for two groups: 1) the very wealthy and 2) the hardy poor people who are already fokked.

Before leaving high school I was convinced by my observations of the illusions of the Teacher's Life that it was the role for me. Some genuinely nice staff treated me much better than I deserved, Jim Thomas, Andrea Jason, and Joe Laz, the night custodian who was around when we rehearsed and built sets for plays. He was a watch repairman, too, which belied his curt treatment of various brooms and vacuums. He taught me you can be classless and still very classy. Fuck class, actually. But not classes.

I cheated a few times in high school. The methods are not important. From this I learned a valuable lesson: students can cheat and trying to stop them may not be productive. Since then, I've hovered and occasionally looked up and around during exams, but I also leave the room, figuring Hey, the cheater's gonna cheat, so let them. Just as I lost by cheating and thus not learning, they would suffer these wages, and put to death their own potential. This is more than "you're only cheating yourself," but it's pretty close.

Eventually it hit me that, my subject being part of the Humanities (sic) [so why are there so many fucked up people in Communication?], I could make the rules for testing. I began passing out copies of the test beforehand, the very thing any student striving for a grade would wish to have, paste the name Study Guide on top, and let them work it over for a few days in the run up to test day. A remarkable note: the # of fails did not change, the # of D's and C's was slightly lower but still chubby, and the # of B's went down while the # of A's went up. This is a nonscientific analysis, but the first part is the notable one: students who don't give a fuck still don't give a fuck when you give them the test beforehand. One semester I even passed out the test WITH ANSWERS. Still there were fails, and the usual distribution held up well. Huh. Is there a lesson here? Even when one facilitates the most advanced form of cheating possible (stealing the test) the results do not change much.

This allowance for reckless flexibility in course design comes with age and tenure and most of all with the culture of college teaching that somehow finds sense in allowing people who could not legally teach first grade to teach university. The professor need only know the subject, and the more that is evident, the capacity to share it in a way that ends up in learning is a mystery.

I swear on Peter Ladefoged's grave (should there be one) that I've been handed "the book" for a course I never took in school and directed to prepare to teach it starting "next week." Yes, one can argue that a true professor can manage such a thing, and learn so quickly that what might take a normal human 16 weeks one can pull off in a weekend. We are so splendid that way. Not really. We can read fast and scan even faster. We've got colleagues who know how to write a Table of Contents (detailed versions, too) that facilitates the writing of syllabi by persons who've not read the meat of the book.

So, me passing out the test on some flimsy theory that people will learn just as much as guessing what I'm going to ask is not only allowed, it's encouraged by the utter freedom a professor has to do just about anything in class. I once heard of a professor who pinched the balls of select students as part of some sort of deep demonstration of something super insightful. And outside of class, it is assumed we are always working and thus it appears that oftentimes we are not. This is an illusion. If one's business is to think, simply being awake becomes work.

*authenticity is a great thing if you can learn how to fake it.

"Outcomes" is a word that crept into the jargon a few years back and it is one of the funniest of all in the tragic comedy of errors we make striving to prove that learning has occurred. The outcomes of a course may require years, even decades, to take form. They may never come. The insights and aha moments that come and go during a course might be all of such moments, but chances are the "pragmatic paradox" or the "intersectionality of the syntagm and the paradigm" rise into actual knowledge through the constant pestering of NOT having understood during the class itself and the subsequent exposure to an endless string of examples that lead to, much much later, the major *aha*, as if one has finally seen the rabbit's head and the old lady in a hat in the same drawing.

I continue to write as if still in the "we" of the so-called "academy." What a word. What a world. But I am finally safely outside of it and have already reflected that was half my stance before and during. Now fully outside, though, some of the oddities become better focused.

Who can tell the recipe of what makes a class nutritious to a student? The recipe calls for ingredients that are entirely outside the control of the teacher, and barely within their influence. We do not know what is populating the minds of our students. Even a good guess is just a guess. They could be note-taking profusely, nodding at all the right moments, laughing on cue, engaged in thinking about next Christmas or what's for lunch. Are they learning then? Yes, how to fake sincerity, which is a grand lesson one can use without wear.

So, as to the qualification of college teachers to teach, that is somehow determined by other college teachers who also would not be allowed to teach a first grade class. It would be really funny if it had not become so expensive.

The crushing dollar cost raises expectations to a level perhaps no one could meet, but even less likely will a poorly prepared non-teacher who has crept into an obscure corner to study erudition and arcanity while working for peanuts in grad school. Good gawd, though, some of them were damn good, even then. And the good TA might be a good teacher, but it's natural, or the product of a thousand little arrows and and hits and getting by, and they would have to try hard *not* to be good.

As I've said before and may say again, even a shitty teacher can teach a helluva a good class, as long as the student brings in the ingredients necessary to learn around them. Paul Hurley, for example, professor of English, expert in Early American poetry, preferring strong the biographical and close textual schools of criticism, and NOT preferring anyone who was not a little English program pet. I watched the constant autonomic bickering as his body fought itself in the early stages of Parkinson's or some other spasmodic affliction; he was bitter of tongue, tone, and comport. He spoke like a snake who'd just eaten might speak, if it could. He mispronounced my name in more extreme forms all semester so that by the end he simply called roll "Miss Muffet." I raised my hand, dutifully, across the table from him. But goddamn if he didn't talk his way through a poem in a way that moved it from black and white to color. "The frail duration of a flower" comes to mind when I think of his bitter breath. He sucked but I learned.

And from various clowns, bitter because they got into something they found out too late they did not love, and from worn out masters who'd long ago stopped reading, and from fresh newbies who were making shit up out of nothing, I learned. From giraffe man Bob

Trager, how to calm a room of hundreds. From
R Paul Hibbs, the contagious effect of unhurried
energy, and from William Minor, that
"creativity is contagious" even when it is
undisciplined (as he never was.)

July 6, 2020

When I was teaching best I was asking questions. Not just Socratic method, but questions intended to cement textbook concepts, examples, and a shared vocabulary for our objects of study. These were useful years. The best class meeting was one where many people talked, on topic. Easy enough to simply get everyone or nearso to talk, given the volatility of certain popular culture topics. But to work a wedge in so someone just can't help themselves but to speak up, that person whose name you do not know yet because they've never spoken, and now, here in week 10 or 11 (the golden weeks*) the time is right and nigh at once, and they speak up. A person's face changes forever once speech comes out of it. Before the voice happens, it is entirely and too much overflowing with possibilities, all projected by the observer. Once speech is formed, the face become linked to the innards of the person, their sound, their style, their choice among all of the now deceased possibilities.

*Golden Weeks: 10-12 of a 16 week term, midterms distant, finals not yet looming.

That is why masks are going to really take a major chunk out of the ass of speech communication teaching. I'd get me one that was thin as a bride's veil, and yet proven to be sufficiently blocking of the evil magic. So glad I'm retired. Can't imagine trying to learn people's names from the tops of their faces and their eyes. Though other features can be helpful. Pretty sure I'd be fired for one gets away with satire, irony, and teasing with the lower half of one's face every bit as much as the upper half. (The eyes have us all bushwhacked into thinking "it's a visual culture." OK, just try watching TV with no sound.)

Teaching will become "half face to half face"--or would that just be "face?" Woe be to all of them. We shall learn that the mouth means more than the eye, and everything to it. Blind people know if you are smiling based on what your mouth does to your voice, not what their eyes don't do.

I remember being sick, teaching sick, being in rooms with lots of sick people, coughing, sneezing, horking up phlegm balls, or just breathing the ick that the sick incubate and deliver so generously. The motivations to come to class even when ill are partly logical and partly illogical. The logical one is that one will not miss and, ergo, one has a better chance at success. The other is that one is really not going to be asked to do anything too strenuous and just sitting around...how bad could it be? Duh.

Relying on the good sense, focus, discipline, patience, means, and ability of late teens and early 20's to perform consistently and all together--this is a pipe dream worthy of its own pipe. Young people are notoriously free-spirited. They don't like being ordered about, especially when they are the client. Just demanding one take an exam on a given day was coming under fire as racist and oppressive long before COVID kicked up its tendrils. Students love to rebel. Rebellion is what is taught in many classes heretofore. So, are these selfsame libertarian (in theory) professors going to suddenly get religion and begin policing? They will become operators for The System, and woe be to them if they discipline one group more than another, regardless of the behavior in question. Click "another reason to be glad to be retired."

All of the above today emerges because of the huge push to have everyone and their dog wear a mask in public and shared spaces. I surely understand the push and agree with it. Yet a notion being sensible in a public health way does not make it practical in an educational one. What will be required is a hugely accelerated movement in the direction higher ed (and perhaps all of ed) was heading anyway: teaching machines.

Professors will become content creators, erstwhile and just for a while managers of the knowledge stored and shared, amending it as required to maintain funding. Their roles will become similar to the rewriters of history in *1984*. Their "books" will never be printed. Content, however, will appear in abundance and be in high demand, for a while. Then someone will discover that computers are good at compiling "facts" and writing prose (having got their practice in providing sports and financial news). This will slice off yet another duty up til now reserved for professors and people who can type or pay to dictate.

Once the face to face teaching is gone, and the content can be generated from the funded knowledge of humankind, professors and scholars will still compete to be heard, or read. Alas, they will be up against the aggregation, the mass, the corpus, of all symbolically stored human knowledge.

The only thing left, for a while, will be art...

July 12, 2020

The sordid ruminations of last entry aside, the task remains: recount every possible memory of teaching and learning. Whether it all lines up chronologically or via some other rhetorical route is to be seen.

This is no purpose here, just an aim.

Is target shooting rhetorical?

Just shot an email off to my UT professor Lynn C. Miller, whom I have not had contact with by any means for several decades, it seems. She stands out in the top 5 of all teachers for blending ability, field knowledge, and an inviting curiosity and conversational ease--this just as true in the class as out. She adapted James Purdy's "Mr. Evening" and "Goodnight Sweetheart" short stories, using her work with Breen at Northwestern as a starting place, embracing Chamber Theatre and staging traditionally. A good experience.

Though we did exchange kind brief notes in the early 80's, I may have tried to contact her years back and to no avail. Not sure I'd write back to me, either.

At UT, thanks to Paul Gray, another fabulous performance studies professor, I read a mess of Ibsen's plays. Their tightness, with not a wasted syllable, design, a textile weave of entirely common but uncommonly placed particulars--were a lesson in unity. Whether there is useful general wisdom in *A Doll's House* or *Enemy of the People* is not for me to say. Such plays and *The Wild Duck* have allowed me to feel educated on occasion throughout the years. And in life, certain grim lessons are repeated from Ibsen in my mind, though I have not laid eyes on any of the plays in decades. From *Doll's House*: the significance of a closing door. From *Wild Duck*, that a man can sit in his room and plan and think he is doing something, but he is not. And from *Enemy*, that one "ought not wear one's good trousers to a revolution." Or something like that. Oh, and that if one chooses to be the one to say there is a turd in the cistern, even though such news is to the benefit of general health, one still ought to expect to be hated for it as if one had dropped it there oneself.

There is a strange aspect that comes over a room just before a performance. Even an ugly space takes on a thin atmosphere not allowing for gravity, as if the walls, and floor, chairs and ceiling all had their own layer of foggy, translucent and slightly iridescent feathers, ready to move just once and sweep the room away into whatever fantasy was to be played on the stage. People and furniture looked better just before a performance. Life was charged up. This is ritual, performance of literature (musical scores, plays, stories, you know) as ancient as the first gathering where someone tossed a tale-- around much longer than mass, longer than temple, longer than daily prayers. The drama of it. This was true as well for the classroom, a fact unstated but apparently known by nearly everyone. And this may explain why I got none of the predicted shit for playing music at the start of class. The song was that day's national anthem. Any ball game, horse race or political gathering goes best with music to begin. And so it was with class. There was, even in the dingiest rooms I have used for teaching, a peach fuzz of that same luminescent aviary, a mist that disappeared if you looked for it or at it, in every gathering just as class was about to start.

Shit I Used to Say

Every teacher no doubt has a list of things they say a lot. Here are some of mine, a list that may expand as reflection stirs the pond. Some of these things would probably get me fired or cited today, but fuck that. By some miracle I got through it legally intact (but not always in tact.)

When two people would sit near and talk whilst I was trying to Expand the Appreciable Universe* by ranting, I would look at them with my best look of longing admiration, pretend to have a slight hiccup of withheld tearful succor, and say softly, "when two young people fall in love in my classes, that makes my heart grow three sizes*" For decades that got a laugh, even when I said it to two men or two women. One couple was startled and said,

"Oh we're not in love. We're married."

"That's no excuse." I said.

But lately such a line, say 3-4 years ago, stopped seeming safe. What if the two men really were falling in love? And what if they were sensitive about being noticed? What if the two women had just enjoyed a night of physics? Sensitivity, all around us and to some degree at MSU, had grown to such precarious heights.

*appreciable universe, hat tip to H.N.Wieman, *Source of Human Good*   *hat tip to Dr. Seuss and the Grinch

Another thing I remember saying a fair bit would come out on any occasion when a student would explain or question the value of something by saying it was "required." For example, "why did you take this class?" is a good first day question. Many students, most actually, would either pander ("I heard you are fabulous") or explain ("my computer science got canceled") or indict scheduling ("this class fit my work hours because my boss is a douche.") Many would say, "I'm taking it because it is required."

To which, polite to a fault, I would aver, "There is no such thing as a required class."

Looks of doubt, confusion, sympathy.

To clarify, the august professor would note, "College itself is optional. Therefore, everything that happens in it is chosen, not required."

"Yes, but I can't get a degree without college," one might up-pipe.

"Who says you have to go to college?"

"But what if I want to be a doctor?"

"Then choose to go to college to get the thing you want, and enjoy the option."

I guess what it all came down to, and which is something that a young person finds hard to accept (not to understand, but to accept) is that wanting something does not make it a requirement.

That is still a hard thing to remember when one is horny or has a sweet tooth no matter one's age.

Another lapidary phrase I would trot out on occasion enough times to remember was "thank you." I would in the closing years, nearly every day in every class, thank them. Not just for pretending to like the music, but "thank you for coming." Once in a while I'd add, "We here at MSU know you have a choice in institutions and are happy you have chosen us." Flyers liked the allusion.

I would also say a civil "Good Morning" to latecomers. I vaguely recall in earlier years giving the stink eye, or ignoring them in subtle ways that indicated my awareness of their tardiness and that it was bothering my flow. But as far back as I can remember, I have said, no matter how late someone was, "good morning" or "good afternoon"--and not in that snotty way that so many teachers use, wherein acid is poured over the phonemes so that they speak the opposite of what they say. I meant it. I meant "thank you for coming." Things are easier to say when they are not gimmicks. Kind of like how the truth is usually easy to remember. Why shouldn't fucking professors thank their clients?

Being kind in no way predicted, however, that I would accept Shinola in place of real shit. Politically and rhetorically (and this took me way too many years to figure out) being overtly kind based on pragmatism ended up providing the lattice to which demands, discipline, and bluntness could be stacked (as needed.)

Another favorite (perhaps only of mine), was to say after 10-15 minutes of back and forth on this or that topic of currency (I hope most of which were topical but do admit to having been led off the trail by students, vixens and wolves)-

-"We'd better start class." On one occasion that "better start class" (which is code for, "I had a plan here somewhere,") would be uttered 5 minutes before the period ended. Shocking what professors are allowed to get away what with Freedom and all.

I was so nice to latecomers that a fellow who came in 30 minutes late (to a 50-minute class) regularly and who came on time just once in four months still got the hearty "Good Morning." And he didn't seem to notice anything strange at all and managed to get right into the business at hand.

My forgiveness for lateness was based on two things: 1) other students would give them enough feedback of the discouraging kind and 2) life is so fucked up that I was amazed anyone ever showed up.

That's another thing I said a lot, (without the "fucked up") in more abundance over the last 10 years: "Thank you for coming. For overcoming gravity. For choosing levity, which is its opposite. For not letting the dozen things that drew you back and away from achieving victory. You overcame all of that and are here."

On occasion one would seem amazed to have accomplished it. But that brought me to a related axiom, oft-uttered, that itself was linked to "no required class" and that was, "College is a choice, and you chose to come. Let's get busy."

There was, then, implicit valuation of their attendance, which itself explained my ranting, prancing, exercising, exorcising, educing, invoking, assigning, provoking (dare I?) It was all there to honor that they showed up, chose us, chose this class and this day to attend it. None of that was bullshit.

I knew then and know now how my paycheck got signed. Though it wasn't purely pragmatic in that sense. I also remembered and still remember student days: the onus of class attendance, and the thousand impediments that had to be overcome to get there and to "attend" in mind as well. It's both hellish and lovable.

Another thing I liked to say when people would give me general shit about how fucked up our language is, "Hey, I didn't invent English or how to speak it."
This came up a bit when the differences between "welts" and "whelps" was germane to the discussion.

A line I stated very often to advisees about working (aka being able to eat) was one I learned by watching people and working in 5 states: "If you are willing to move, you'll have a job."

No one ever came back and said, "you were wrong about that." But that could be because they starved to death on the Oregon Trail.

Funny how things you only say once can have monumental impact. To wit, my future wife-to-be was a student of mine in the summer of 1998, the lovely Allison Forman. Our eventual coming together made way to discuss things we had noticed about one another, and she said something that got her attention was when I stopped teaching (aka "ranting") to stoop down to tie a shoelace, saying, "I can't think right when one shoe is tighter than the other." Apparently this spoke to her on several levels, and she got the notion we might be future kin.

She was right. We've been married nearly 20 years.

Never said that about shoes before or since. Hadn't occurred to me before and I don't need more than one wife at a time.

As I peter out on today's writing, nostalgia creeps in about what is past and passed. The past has always been out of reach except for whatever illusions one manages to retain, comparing on occasion to the illusions of those who were there at the time. But the "passed," which I spent perhaps too much time eulogizing last entry, is that un-cautious, completely free, unprocessed class experience--perhaps the final truly free speech community we've had. I am pretty sure we've lost it. People are being fired for saying sensible things that ought to be treated as propositions for debate rather than bases for cancellation.

July 13, 2020

One year ago I started this missive to no one and everyone and to myself in a most naive predicament. It is a predicament because there was no way out and there is no way out. We simply cannot see or even imagine what's coming. That is not only a General Axiom but a current description. Glimmers of changes, all to affect changes in education, are afoot. Economic, technological, political, social, legal, international, environmental: an avalanche.

I am drawn to consider those even though my aim here is to remember. Let's do that first, and along the way, once again, tangents may develop that allow me to leave a bit of a bread trail post-covid. With millions ill, hundreds of thousands dying, and no clear end in sight as to immunity of any kind, with mutations looming, education strives to press on.

There are the teachers, presumably the most valued cog in the wheel, and administrators, who have lives that require 3 or 4 times as much money to sustain as teachers. Those two groups tend to average older and more vulnerable to the virus. Many of them want to stay away from kids, known to be nearly invulnerable and due to their proclivities, likely to be handy Super Spreaders, our current equivalent of Typhoid Mary. Teachers and administrators that would prefer to stay away from kids are a strange match to what education requires: closeness.

Every now and then over the last 40 years a student would come along that felt close to me. This has nothing to do with sex and is a valid feeling, as I have had it. For Michelle McShane, for Mrs. Collins, for Mr. Jensen (that knowing twinkle), for Roderick Gordon, Ted (whose last name escapes me now and is proof of the need for these memories to be scratched down), Professor Ted who was neck deep in existentialism, which itself had become institutionalized and thus bedridden. For James Van Oosting and Marvin Kleinau and his a little bit scary smart professor and wife Marion, for

116

Judy Little, the meek poet with fangs and talons, for Lynn C. Miller, Paul Gray, all tending toward the literary side of college and life, for so many I cannot recall by name to name--I've had this closeness. Sometimes it would lead to uncomfortably long pauses in their offices, once the immediate matter had been attended to, as I grew comfortable simply being there near such minds and intellects, that their human sides would begin to wonder at the reason, motivation, or proclivity that was causing me to visit and to linger. This I have experienced as a teacher, too, and remembered it, learned it was not intimate closeness of the kind the bodies of the world crave, but a perceived intellectual *esprit de corps*, sought but not hunted, desired but not expected.

This develops between "colleagues" on faculties, too, but to name those with whom I felt immediate *hnau** would interrupt the flow here...

*see Lewis: *Out of the Silent Planet*

Some students would come to talk, and talk, and talk. During the final semester (or half of one) a former student stopped by regularly at 9:55am Monday, Wednesday, and Friday. He was a high frequency, low-labor visitor, as I do believe he would have been happy for me to say a little less than I did when I could work a turn into the conversation. The context was familiar to me: a student digs a course (is it the course or

the teacher or both?) does not matter why. Is lit
up intellectually somehow. Or even when one's
course simply drops well into a schedule that
begins to reveal a synthesis across and between
subjects, the student needs to talk to someone
they already know thinks like they do. Chicken
or egg, the professor's ears (and the mind
assumed to lie between them), are invaluable.
For a while, anyways. He was showing no signs
of slowing his visits, which was fine with me,
but the Rona kicked us all out of the world.

Intelligent students, mature students (for
their age), students who'd lived through more in
a month that I had in a year as to suffering and
loss. Students with wild ideas who need ears
that seem to listen: the one who was going to get
venture capital so he could design and build a
power generation plant run by the heat and
movement of the thermal features of the
earth...the one who was convinced he would be
a writer whom I thought needed to spend as
much time writing as he did talking...the masters
candidate working through, out loud, the
meanderings that lead to an idea and thus to a
thesis...To all of them I probably talked too
much and listened too little. The hazard of
asking a professor to be one's sounding board.
Some of them needed a lot of help getting past
pauses. Others really didn't much need me, but
a professor in an office listening is (as we have

learned since March) a very large part of what one purchases when one goes to college.

The classroom, then, is really not where all of the teaching takes place. As the Nez says, the master lets the student win on occasion. This happens in hallways, offices, on sidewalks, in grocery stores, on the dam at the wide end of Eagle Lake, anywhere. In this sense the professor is "never off."

What a feller needs to know how to do, though, besides endure the travails and torments of listening so much, is to know when the student needs to see someone else. There have been times when the student asks to close the door (properly so)--a practice that has become too hazardous in the last 10 years so I stopped doing it--but these closed door matters are important and can easily stray out of the purview of today's Shackled Professor. Some needed to see a counselor, some the police. Some needed expert medical advice or legal guidance. Some needed to get home and work things out and come back (and it was OK for a prof to say as much out loud). A few needed a hug, and some got one until all touching was sexualized by morons. A few needed just to cry, to lay out what had been happening to a semi-strange ear.

Don't get the idea that I spent time counseling. Advising maybe. Counseling, no. I always diverted that to the professionals on campus. These counseling people might rank among some of the most fucked up individuals in the world, (I really do not know them all, but the ones I do suggest a trend...) but they do have credentials. To say that a professor's life is not one of frequent counsel would be wrong, and that is where one's metaphysics and politics can very easily blow strong. Much caution needs to be exercised. If one believes in what one does, then how else could it be?

Students in class would probably have a hard time pinning me down into religious, ethnic, geographic (OK, "northern"), or political camps. That's good. But students who visited the office might get a bit more of those things. In the classroom, they're on my time. In the office, I'm on theirs. So I can shoot the mouth off a little more.

Or, as one should do ever more often in the classroom: listen.

Might be that an attentive professor is among the first adults to treat the student AS an adult. This new experience for them has a lot of appeal, and the shine takes a while to wear off. The professor abides the wait.

Reflections on student office encounters:

Texas, 1980: in the wee office I shared with two other Grad Assistants. We were helping professors with their classes while we also taught 1 or 2 of our own. I was busy at my desk by the door when a student from Hopper's class came in carrying his recent exam paper. I invited him to sit and talk and he lurched into an argument that went something like this.

"You graded my paper low because I'm black."

I said, "How's that?"

"You scored me lower because I am black." People often repeat things as if repetition improves a claim.

"How could I know you were black? Have we met before today?"

"I think you're saying that because I'm white."

He paused, adjusted his mind to that, and politely left.

Hampton Institute, (an HBCU, founded by Samuel C. Armstrong, Union officer in 1868, presently Hampton University,) 1983: Penny S___ comes in, looking pent up. She sits across from my desk (I didn't arrange the place--I never would have put a desk between me and the client) and began to express her concerns:

"Mr. Modaff, some of the others and I in your class find your use of humor to be too much." She was very polite but firm with tinges of rehearsal.

"I do try to keep things light (a racist metaphor?) What is the problem?"

"We think your jokes are so frequent as to diminish the seriousness of the class. Particularly certain jokes."

I reflected on some of my more insane commentary and immediately saw where she was coming from up 'til then, but there was more:

"You see, we expect that you might not take us seriously, given your race. So, when you use so much humor, that seems to confirm that expectation." She may not have been quite that polysyllabic, but she was close.

"I do joke a lot."

"Yes, you do."

"But let me ask you something."

"OK."

"If I was not white, would we be having this conversation?" A sincere question, not a Socratic trap in the least.

"Probably not."

"So while I tone down my humor as much as I can and still be me, will you consider that the color of my skin--which was not my choice--has played a role for you as well in this moment?"

This was before the current movements and immediate assumptions of white racism, yet whites were expected by even the young, surely through repeated experience and observation, to dog blacks as much as possible, including not taking them seriously. And whites were victims of these expectations. So when a white behaved (as I did with my humor) in any sort of way indexing this frame of mind, Penny and others would assume it was just a white guy being white and thus an asshole.

They did not know that I joked around just as much in a classroom full of whites. This is the piece that she missed. A little broadening of context often helps. (See Epictetus' *Enchiridion*.)

Still, there should be a little laughter in a serious matter such as a white man presuming to stand up in front of a classroom full of black students and do any sort of teaching.

Lesson learned.

My last term there, Penny, now a senior, with huge smile took occasion to say in front of a class she was in that I had "come a long way" and that she was glad to know me. Gosh. How did that happen? Well... she made a good point, I had changed. And I had made a good point: she thought it over and gave me a chance as an individual--not as a white.

July 14, 2020

I did fall asleep a time or two at my desk in Breckinridge Hall at MSU. On some jobs falling asleep would be shameful, even deadly. Professoring ain't like driving a locomotive with a half mile train behind it. Quarter mile, maybe.

Not sure if anyone ever saw me sleeping. I like to think I was good enough at sensing an approach, and my office (until the final 3 semesters) was favorably located at the end of a hallway near which only the windowless door to an unused closet was in view from my desk chair. That changed when space got tight and some graduate student assistants were installed in the closet that had been filled once with the paper makings of *The Trail Blazer*, MSU's student newspaper. Once those grad students were going in and out, visual notice opportunities increased dramatically, and I had to perform busy-ness with ocular and well as auditory vigor.

Asleep now and then, yes, but I was THERE. As a light sleeper, one finds a ready excuse: "I wake quickly." This is also handy when driving.

This July 2020 evening I care not to write about much but my time teaching in the prison. I believe the incident, already shared, leading up to my standing ovation was the most dramatic thing that occurred, but there are other memories and oddly (un)comfortable moments---

What? I forgot to tell you about my one and only standing O? Well!
After being asked back to the prison to finish out the class, I returned with a bit of a jaunt in my step, making sure to exit my car only once, and made my way to the chapel wherein our class had so rudely been interrupted by jaded fuckheads following orders.

I entered, the class was in position, in their usual seats. With no apparent prompting, like a flock of birds whirling they rose from their seats and leapt into vigorous applause. I think they did it so loudly because they knew if it lasted too long a guard would come (if there even was one on the wing, which there often was not.) We were, one believed and hoped, surveilled.

Smiling bigly, setting down my teacher wares (folders, nothing zipped or closable), I waited. Very soon they stopped and took their seats in somewhat less orderly fashion, looking up for the first words...

"So--" I began, eyes out among them as if making sure that they were all there.*

"--where were we?"

Laughter, clapter, and the opening of books.

They knew the whole story before I did, looks like. My return was as much a victory for them as it was a thing to admire, as it appeared that I had flipped a wee bird toward the windmill and won.

THEY knew who Don Quixote was.

*where else would they be?

The incarcerated students were among the best I've encountered out of the 8500+ in 40 years. (Let this be a lesson in the utter disconnection between being intellectual facile and thoroughly moral.) They had plenty of time to study, as the joke went. To them, college was no laughing matter. They dared to step out of "population" and go to school. They could lose the privilege (enjoyed by interned persons of all colors) at the drop of a hat or a crowbar. They had to work, too. And the pay was about 85 cents an hour. They gave the best speeches (with a few regular schmalzers.) Memorable topics:

Why the Federal Government Should Stay off of Private Farmland

End the War On Drugs by Taking the Money and Simply Buying All the Drugs

How to Buy A Good Winter Coat

New Crimes the State Can Execute People For (1994-ish crime bill)

Getting Published In Prison (Lou T______, prolific lifer)

Knot Tying (no nooses)

They seemed to take each other seriously as audience members and speakers. A feller still had to watch what he said, as Lou T___ made clear one week.

The previous week Lou had made a comment during one of his speeches about Kentucky men who were married to women much bigger than them. Something along the lines of, "you see them tagging along behind their woman, slumped and skinny in their boots behind a mama four times bigger wearing bigger boots."

He apologized frankly and thoroughly the next week. I can only imagine the conversations folks had had with him in the interim.

I learned a new phrase in the prison-- "trick bag." A trick bag is trouble, generally speaking.

Specifically it refers to someone giving you something like a sow's ear and calling it a purse. To continue the porcine metaphor, it's a pig in a poke. A trick bag can be a grift or a sneak. In any case, one ought not allow oneself to "be handed one." I can't remember who it was, Lou or somebody during one of the breaks, "don't let anybody hand you a trick bag." That may have been his way of offering to watch out for me. Another term was "pill call" referring to a trip to the infirmary.

The deficit of uniforms (as in oftenly none) on the wing did on occasion make me nervous. That is, until I realized the guards were way more scary than the residents.

Lou

Lou Torok was a published author, an intellectual, knew Ezra Pound's *ABC of Reading* better than I, and a thrice convicted child molester doing life. I didn't know what his crime was (or anyone's) while I was working there. Never asked and folks almost never offered. A radio interview featuring Lou aired years later wherein he casually admitted why he was in prison for life. I suppose if one wants to clarify the reason for a life sentence, being a child molester might somehow ease the mind in place of murderer. But not much. The other guys didn't seem too warm toward him, but they did admire him, I think, because he was so fucking smart.

For several years after I stopped going there we corresponded via snail mail. Envelopes from Lou were, of course, opened before I got them. And everything I sent to him got the same treatment. He listened to me on the radio and warned me about being too frank about things and to keep the audience in mind. Perhaps he sensed as I did that the only difference between some of the convicts and me was that they got caught.

No, I was never a child molester, but surely there were a few moments (having nothing to do with sex) when other things were going on that would have turned out badly if the police had happened by. Overtly, I respected the incarcerated students as men who were clamped down (most often rightfully) by the state, but were willing to claw up a little by getting a degree in prison. Inwardly, I was just praying they wouldn't kill me, or worse yet, turn me over to the guards. Clients were always addressed as "Mister___" by me.

Lou once sent to my office at MSU a letter with a newspaper clipping inserted. It was one of the many newspaper features that had been done on him over the years. People were impressed by his catalog of writings and his vigor. He was mid 70's at the time and had no prospect of ever being free. He deserved what he got. In the face of all of that, he continued to have a rich, vast symbolic life. Two things he said can be recalled, and one of them was written on the article he slipped into his letter.

The photo was taken through his open cell door, a lone window high in the shot, overexposed, Lou in the near dark, almost a silhouette, typing away on his newsletter, or another inspirational book, or who knows what. And scrawled in the white space of the newsprint, by the overexposed window (which hid the bars well), these words appeared:

"Wish you were here. Lou"

He knew how to turn a cliche into poetry. Fucking child molester. Think what he might have done if he hadn't done that. Then again, perhaps it was prison that unlocked whatever artist was locked up in him.

The other memorable thing he said was a comment in class as I was waxing with febrile rhetorical aplomb about how a speech should have the rise and fall of a story, following Aristotle. And if it did not, I averred, then as Pound said (from his perch in the madhouse) the utterance becomes a "slushy mass of rhythm."

Lou piped up and added, astutely, "a slushy mass of rhythm and *tone*." He even did a melodic shift on "tone." I was blown away that he even knew who Pound was, but did not signal such, for quoting Pound to begin with was foolish, except perhaps to me and to Lou.

For years I walked around believing that I had misquoted Ezra Pound that day, and that the word "tone" had been omitted. But just last year or so I dug out *ABC of Reading,* just to see what the fuck. Turns out we were both wrong. But he was righter than I was.

The actual quote goes like this:

"Music in the past century of shame and human degradation slumped in large quantities down into a soggy mass of tone." (Treatise on Meter, *ABC of Reading*)

Damn.

At the prison when I started teaching there, the jolly Susan A_______ ran the academic wing. She was a battle axe in defense of the State giving prisoners an education. She had kickass stats that made the case for keeping people from returning to prison by teaching them something while they were in it. She was so damn good that, of course, she got kicked upstairs to the capitol and was replaced by the aforementioned scrotum who had me run out of the place (for 4 days) due to the fingerprinting incident.

At one of our visits the topic of life in the region came up, and thus what was special about its people. She said it had been no problem adjusting for her (I figured that would be true even on a pirate ship), but her husband had encountered some difficulties. He was of middle eastern origins, and looked it. Well, seems that one day he was riding his bicycle in West Liberty, KY (where the prison, without the batting of an eyelash as to the cruel irony, was located...) and some gentlemen of what was probably local birthright drove their truck along side of him and shouted unkind words and perhaps launched a mostly empty beer bottle or two.

Believe it or not, one could be any color and get that sort of treatment riding a bicycle in Eastern Kentucky. That's just how more than the usual number of folks feel about adults riding bicycles, for reasons we may get into another time. But if you're *expecting* to be hassled because you are not from a place, then rude comments and beer bottles take on a more menacing patina than mere bicylophobia. Therefore, the harangued husband chose to report the abuse to the local sheriff.

According to Susan, the sheriff, after listening to the tale, smiled a bit and completely free of guile said,

"Well don't worry. They probably though you was a n___r."

Come to think, that might have been part of what motivated her to help herself *get* kicked upstairs to Frankfort where, I understand, one has to do more than ride a bicycle to get such abuse.

July 16, 2020

Hot today. Hot hot. Humid and hot. Hottest day so far. And this chases people indoors to a place where the experts say the Rona is more catching than ever. Cases on the rise. Deaths on the rise, but the mortality rate drops as more cases that are not fatal are logged. Opinions range from "the entire thing is a hoax" to "it's the End of the World." The end of the world may be a hoax, but the entire thing is a mess of historic proportions. So with the heat and the isolation, I am driven once again to this seat, and the ongoing reflections on teaching and learning...

One of the duties of a professor is to review the writing of others. Grading (which we will consider later on), document review for administrative duties, records for and by students relating to matriculation (one of the dirtiest-sounding words in the educational lexicon), memos, ads, mass emails, and on and on. (I don't give a fuck about ending with a preposition--they're usually right on).

One writing chore a professor is not required to do but can accept is the review of textbooks. Often a prof will get an email inviting review of a chapter or a few chapters of an upcoming new book, or the most recent revision. I've done a handful of these over the years, and on occasion this little extra $ bonus has been well timed. One such review stands out above all of the others for what it taught me about myself and about the hideous innards of academic publishing.

The book in question was Charles L___'s *Persuasion*, now printed in its 13th edition. The edition I was commissioned to review was the 13th, as I had just used the 12th. This revealed what a shameful ass I had become as a teacher and even worse how horrid the book had become as a book intended for college students. Ugh.

I thought I knew this book well. It had been used by the student me in my undergraduate years. I must admit that since I'd later used the book in several of its editions at various schools and in teaching several classes, there was a confidence in the 12th edition that led me to a regrettable action: I adopted and used it without reading every word or the footnotes. As I was to find out when reviewing the 13th edition draft, when one dared to actually read every word, a nightmare quickly developed.

Let me apologize to the world for not reading the 12th edition as closely as I should have. That would have led me to apologize to my Persuasion students many dozens of times for selecting a book so rife with errors. Suffice it here to say that in the 13th edition draft there were hundreds of errors in spelling, punctuation, diction, juxtaposition, and factual content. I marked the photocopy they sent me with detailed corrections and notes and, to clarify what some of the marginal notes meant, did a 14 page single-spaced annotated summary and explication.

Laws were misnamed. Dates were wrong. Captions read the wrong names of some of the famous people pictured. Examples were inserted that did not fit, but appeared to have been additions of "current" material that were more like political tirades (and thus already dated) than useful exemplars. It was a mess. Beyond embarrassing. Beyond intolerable. Criminal, in fact, that students were charged to own it. They should have been paid reparations for having been required to buy it in the first place. Thank God none of them read much of it or my pants would have been pulled down.

How does this happen? *Persuasion* was one of the most widely-used college textbooks on the subject. That's right. Larson profited well. The 13th edition is still selling for over $100 in paperback. The author deserved fat payment for the first few editions, no doubt. It was once a solid book. But the numerous and frequent revisions had each led the content further from facts and accuracy. Publishers job out editing and revisions for editions of established books. Clearly, people who do not know the subject are turned loose to either edit themselves or hire yet another jobber to do it. Perhaps a sweaty steam room in a far-off land is filled with competent English speakers who are hired by someone who hired someone to do what they were hired to do. In any case, their work was a mess.

They had more than 1000 people being killed in 1996 in OK City. The real number was 168 (though there was an unidentified left leg.)

They called Bush's famous "No Child Left Behind" education reform act "Leave No Child Behind." Misnamed the Apollo astronauts. And on and on.

The editorial team somehow countenanced the author's "new material" inserts (which stuck out like a clay pecker on an ivory statue) that were nothing more than dated political rants and inside jokes only flaming liberals would appreciate.

And for this people were charged > $100.

Prof L__ no doubt staggered in glee all the way to the bank each time he got his royalty checks.

Taught me a lesson or some:
1. READ the goddamn book; every word
2. DON'T use textbooks if you can help it.
3. Some major Publishers give not a fuck about accuracy and editorial flair.
4. Money is cool, but it can stink sometimes when attached to such a mess.
5. Add a zero when quoting a job in editing. I got 500. Should have got 5000.

As for the more common form of editing a professor does, there is...

On Grading

I'm tempted to be completely honest about grading and what it devolved into as my time teaching drew to a close. Without a doubt it is the thing I spent the most time doing, thinking about, worrying about, enduring, and possibly earning my paycheck. Grading was also trench warfare between two sides of my mind, the procedural/political and the idealistic/rational. (Or, Tom Pace, the eidetic.)

My experiences as a student with grading taught me the gravity grades can have for some people. (Some could not give less of a shit even if a thing called "negative shit" were invented.) The grades I carried home on my own "report card" in elementary could mean ease or punishment, glory or goat. Early school years the grade reports included "conduct marks"-- these were the most horrifying, the place where the Teacher had control over the tenor of one's fate. True power.

That such power was never attractive to me I can claim without fabrication. On occasion I did let the pen slip up or down pushed by some things that had nothing to do with the "rubric." (Oh God don't get me started on rubrics.) Did I know the person's name? Did I know their face? Did I know their voice? All of this could influence how something was read by this grader. Did the graded ever visit the office? Express any form of motivation or interest? Have they shared conditions in their life that modify how their accomplishment appears (in spite of or because of conditions, e.g.)? All of these actual things are not factual things in relation to (a) what the assignment was and (b) if the object conforms or not.

So if one wishes to explain grading one must explain assignments.

Simple enough just to call everything a prof asks students to do for a score an "assignment." Tests, essay, quizzes, talks, exercises, anything. Assignments.

It is *grading* that makes an assignment an assignment.

Objective Tests

Objective tests are the easiest way to remove nearly everything that is unpleasant about grading. There is an answer, every time. And the teacher can defend the answers' correctness if need be, should a student seek to differ as to the "right one." Grading these exams is easy. Machines can and do it. But composing them well is hard. The discretion vulnerable to influence by what one thinks of the students in the class is exercised when composing an objective test, unlike with an essay exam.

Subjective Tests

Sure, this is a fair phrase to describe the opposite of objective. Connotation is not helpful, though, as "subjective" has come to mean, at least over the last 50 years or so, something that is unreliable, prone to idiosyncrasy, free from the requirements of sense. Such connotations are unfortunate but might describe the act of grading an essay of any kind.

Yes, the "rubric" might specify some things the grader will be looking for. If a student provides all of these rubricized things evidently enough for the teacher to notice, the rubric has been served and the grade may be high. Alas, there is the other paradigm that is operating in an essay, the paradigm laid out by the writer's mind, the thing their diction serves.

Now we *could* grade only on diction and avoid the whole mind thing. But who is able?

Saying yes to "I will read as if listening to thoughts," means slowing things down a bit. Reading is not proofreading or cue-eyeballing anymore. The true "subjectivity" of the subjective essay is appertained. And it's tiring.

Woe is us, poor overpaid teachers (or not). This is the ditch digging, the gravel shoveling, the weed pulling, the pitch-forking of the profession: subjective grading.

Now what will a professor do when bravely reading thoughts? Find some appealing mainly because consonant with their own? Or find some revolting because of dissonance? If one is mindful and pert, the dissonance might become the root of deeper reading of oneself even as one objects to the essay. Is this not a function that the offensive writing made possible? Should we not reward the student who writes thoughts contrary to our own?

But what of the grade...professor?

When the dissonance is with facts established and widely known, another obligation, less self-centered, comes into play: correcting.

We are all familiar with correction. Red marks on misspellings. Crossed out numbers

140

and symbols. Formatting errors noted. Errors are corrected.

Yet when the fact averred by the student is contrary to the widely known and accepted version of history (for when is conflict not about history and history about conflict?) an obligation kicks in not only to mark the error, but to correct it with an explanation.

Long before the recent spate of riots (which seem never ending depending on how one defines "riotous"), many years ago a student used in his speech the case of Michael Brown, whose death inspired a certain protest slogan that had buried within it an incorrect version of what occurred. The student spoke as if the officer had been convicted and prosecuted for murder. A perversion of the facts. This Caucasian student found the Brown case useful in a broader argument he was making, but how could I let such an error slide by, nodding or sleeping along with the other 24 people in the room? So, during the usual analytical discussion following the talk, I said something like this:

"Mr. ___ you need to check the facts more closely and broadly. The local grand jury ruled the shooting legally justified and the documented facts contradict the Hands Up Don't Shoot story. Also, the Department of Justice of the United States ruled the same in the Michael Brown case."

Silence. Mildy foggy nod. The whir of gears possibly putting me in the Racist drawer. Silence from the class. No one said, "yeah, I read that, but it was in the *National Enquirer*." Even that would have been preferable to silence. Did they not care? Were variations on the fundamental facts of an event, otherwise known as alternate narratives, not important, even when they became the dishonest (and thus crippling) bases for a movement?

This part of grading, "evaluating," does not always happen with a pen in one's hand (or a cursor.) And it does not always receive a warm welcome.

I wonder if I said precisely those words in class today if I'd have a job a week later.

Subjectivity was the topic tonight in this excursion, as in "subjective grading." One's own thoughts, experiences, memories, reading ability all blend into this analytical auger (or augur) through which assertions made by students are run. How could it *not* be this way? Possibility: Only if one is grading by scanning for objectively identifiable forms and nothing more.

Every case of mistaken facts did not get corrected by me. I must have missed loads of bullshit that sounded convincing and that I had no time to check. And, because I did not know differently, the only version there was to consider was the version provided by the

142

student in her or his talk. This is why, particularly if teaching speech or rhetorical communication, a broad knowledge of topics and subjects is useful. Because no one can know everything, (not even Curie), there will be gaps.

In the case of the HandsUpDon'tShoot wrongful slogan, I asked myself before bringing up the error, "does this matter?" I had no idea at the time how powerful a condensation symbol Mr. Brown's death would become, even to this day, nor how tenaciously the complete bullshit tale about how he died would endure. The wrong story was cemented tightly in the minds of safe white people taking a stand for the hapless POC.

Who is one to decide which errors should be corrected and which should be endured, particularly when uttered aloud in the class itself? If one does not comment on an obvious error, one is complicit in lengthening its lifespan. Just as true, one takes a risk daring to correct any error, more-so lately, because of the new foreground of privilege and power. Who are YOU to say that the introduction of a speech should come first, anyway?

Tween

Between objective and subjective is the space the professor must abide if teaching a full load of courses all of which include writing assignments. One scans both for the objectively defined rubrical requirements, and tracks for the most grievous errors at the same time. This makes living possible. For if one were to give the full measure of consideration to each paper, grading a single assignment would take up all of the time between classes where such things as naps are meant to occur.

Exceptions
    Sometimes a student demolishes or dismisses the rubric in some way or all ways, and this should not always lead to an F, nor did it for me every time. If the quality of what the submitted in place of what was requested was in some way extraordinary, why not? If it did appear to have been written for my class, but just took a hard turn after the title, some credit was still due. At least that's what I remember thinking in the bucolic, gregarious final years.
    Rose ___ a theatre student in my speech class back in the early 1990's, approached her persuasive speech assignment with next to no regard for the particulars of the rubric. In what was probably an excerpt or blending of scripts she knew, she began as if steeling herself for her thesis statement, but then wearily sat down and told a tale of personal woe that established her as experienced in the matter, whatever that was. The room was spellbound. I was hearing nothing of evidence, documentation, warrants,

grounds, etc. And yet, even though all of those were missing, her captivating telling of a personal tale did (if we went along) contain nothing *but* facts, ample expertise, and sound documentation, however limited each of these were when emanating from just one source: her. Still, if one accepted her first premise "I've set my speech aside simply to tell you the truth," she hit every one of the requirements in a manner or two.

But what I *wanted* to say to her was:

"OK hotshot, we're gonna see what kind of soldier you are."

July 19, 2020

Forgive me, I may be repeating what I've described in an earlier section. Sometimes it's on purpose... The advantage to you will be the same as patience during the retold tales of the elderly, who with each telling add or omit some detail that reframes all prior telling and sets up future ones. Ahh, truth, Lawrence D__ alas, resides in four volumes.

One of the areas of power professors have: said power being rooted in existing as a committee of one in most course decisions, is the selection of textbooks and readings.

We ought not let the current explosion of publication sully the corpus of what has come before. While nothing of the quality of *Philosophy in a New Key* is likely being produced today, chances are, if it was, it would be lost in the fierce, shore-eating tides of other waves, identity politics, and simple over-profusion.

One could once suffice to be profound. Now one needs mainly to be profuse. Some are, on occasion, profusely profound.

As Richard L___ once said at a brown-bag lunch meeting of grad students and tenured professors: the first question administrators are going to ask after congratulating you for your latest book being published is, "So, what's next?"

Among the blasting, worldwide textual profusion today, what does/can a professor choose for students to read in, say, a public speaking class? Transcripts of great women's speeches? Aristotle on *Rhetoric*? Lippmann? Helen Keller? Is the traditional association of the word "text" with the written word in need of servicing? Are media recordings not texts? If so, the "assigned reading" in a communication course probably ought to include lots of media. Transcripts just don't cut it. If they did, people would not pay to go to the theatre.

And a class is a play. Of all kinds.

One can have one's genitals petted by a conga line of textbook publishers if one wishes to stand still long enough to listen to them talk. They are not just selling a textbook. They are selling media archives, quizzing apps, pre-fab tests, online grading, student performance uploading and evaluations apps, and on and on.

Oh, and a "book" which is a digitized, hypertexted version (or perversion) of what once was merely printed on paper. When one buys certain textbooks today, one buys an entire, ready-made course. When I think of bakeries (and is there a bad one?), I admit the value of having someone else do certain things (like pastry). But letting the online machine built by a publishers of a "textbook" build one's own course?
That is plain surrender.

People do it. Thus they have invited the camel's nose, The Teaching Machine, aforementioned, into the tent. Excuse me, "the Academy." (Cue barf.)

'Tis not hypocritical for me to make fun of the phrase The Academy whilst just having finished 43 years there as college teacher and student. The referent is fine. The phrase is silly. People say it like they say "The Meadowlands." This is not an equation. I could burn up pages and advance arthritis today just bleating and bragging on my teachers for what they chose for us to read, as I used some of it myself. But in the interest of using what time remains before my death most productively, I shall share those few titles that I can remember which students commented upon favorably.

The best comment on an assigned reading is the immediate and ambitious discussion of the ideas put forth in it. No time is wasted

148

questioning whether we wasted our time reading it. *Enchiridion*, from Epictetus, is one such work. Attributed to his students' class notes as he taught, his "handbook" is a raw, witty treatise on Stoicism in practice. Heard about it in my SIU-C 1979 course Problems in Modern Philosophy. The lethargic but unintentionally clever professor assigned this ancient work. Go figure. It was a good read then, and it's a good read now. Point here is, the students did not hesitate to agree strongly with parts and to disagree strongly with other parts. All I had to do was set them to hunt the text to find instances of each. No problem. What it added up to was admiration and some derision for his assumptions. Because this exercise was done in a Conflict & Communication course, a valuable lesson emerged: it is OK to admire some of what someone says while noting they are full of shit on other matters.

[Rest here. Get yourself a drink.]

July 20, 2020

To avoid going to the store (and thus presumably to avoid contracting the dreaded coronavirus) we've been ordering online here at home for delivery. Today, duct tape arrived. I bring this up only because it relates to voice and articulation, a subject I taught for many years, the first two of which passed even though I'd no formal training in the subject. THAT was one of those classes where the teacher had better be a fast reader (and love phonetics).

Anyhow, people call it "duck tape" because they overlap the final [t] of duct with the initial [t] of tape. Natural assimilation. To properly cite the words "duct tape" with 2 [t]'s in conversation would get one a look most times. So, we all excuse the blend, and a company even decided to go whole hog and started calling itself Duck Tape, complete with a duck logo.

The only sad part about that derivation is that ducts get left in the dark.

Today I am moved to recall moments of succor that a professor is invited to provide. For some reason, when a predicament involving frail bodies presents itself, my heart becomes nearly the heart of a human, and civilized (rather, disciplined) behavior has taken place.

If ever there was a word that deserved to be a preposition, it would be "place," wouldn't it?

Case 1: Epileptics weren't always so well-assisted by their medications. And for some, medicines mean only a lessening, not a cure. I recall one student who said she would know when a seizure was coming, would try to make it out into the hall, would appreciate being watched but not interfered with, and please do call the ambulance. Relaxing instructions. I remember thinking that the hall was not carpeted, a fact which had heretofore only meant that the cleaners had an easier time. She finished the class without us having to exercise her wishes, but I do either dream or recall that she knew on a few days to excuse herself from coming to the room because she felt something afoot and stayed safely home.

Case 2: In a summer class in the year 2000 here at Morehead State I had a student who reported her epilepsy and that often it was undramatic to everyone around her but she still needed support. While sitting one period among the students at the tables, as I did often listening to speeches, presentations, and talks, I felt my right forearm tighten, as if a bundle of snakes had curled about it for a nap. The source was her rigid hand, resting as a grandmother might on her grandchild's arm as they stepped up a curb. I looked away from the speaker and my notes and turned to her, just then noticing she (the one with epilepsy) was seated next to me. Her eyes spoke the paragraph in an instant: *Having one*. We exchanged the look a moment longer and because she remained quiet on the outside. No one seemed to notice her grandmotherly gesture but me, so I turned back to the speaker and eventually she eased up her grip and moved her hand the two inches necessary to fulfill appropriate distancing for strangers at a table.

I do not recall her ever saying Thank You, and I'm glad she did not. Perhaps she did not even remember what happened. That day I learned, even as the teacher, that simply sitting still as a tree is a good thing to practice at times.

No one has vomited in class except my daughter Kelly, when she was but 4 years old or so and attending my 8 a.m. class by some necessity. She warned me it was coming; let's just leave it at that.

Amazing that no college student has hurled in any class I have taught or taken. Shocking, when you consider the malodorous blather that some professors can get into.

Two students out of the 8-9000 I taught passed out in class. One was at Alfred University while I was teaching in the AU TV studio, a fine theatre-like classroom and great place to make useful video recordings of talks. This gentleman evidently had been researching the consumption of adult beverages the night before and had not taken proper measures to engage both body and brain for the morning's classes. As we stood in a circle exercising some fool breathing technique for Voice and Broadcasting, he fell back like a chess piece. His head received grace as it landed on a coiled pile of TV camera cable. Hardly soft, but much preferable to the cement floor beneath it. He didn't feel a thing by then anyway. Ambulance response time: an impressive 7 minutes.

Prognosis: same thing next weekend.

The other person who passed out did so at MSU in the old Room 305 at a time when many people report wishing they could pass out themselves: right before giving a speech. She made it to the front of the room, showing signs of preparation with perhaps just one quick stumble that could be attributed to sole moisture brought in from the rain. At that critical moment the speaker owns the room as anticipation builds, down she goes, taking the chalk rail with her. The rail slowed her fall a bit, and the wall being nearby created enough friction to put her speed at a place where the tile floor wasn't too much of an insult. By that time, though, one notes she was not keeping track of sensations.

I thought, "we're gonna have to get that rail fixed," but I said, "Hey _____ can you run next door to my office and call EMS?" (pre cell phone era)

Superb response time: 4.5 minutes.

Verdict: she, too, had an academic bone for studying the bottom of a glass.

Speeches

Though it was nearly all of 40 years ago, I remember a particular speech very well, one given at the august institution: The University of Texas at Austin. I can't believe they ever let me in the state, much less into that place, but hey, there I was, teaching a class in Public Speaking to that variegated cross-section of the student body known as General Education. A thin, blond, pseudo-Amishly skirted woman of 19 or

20 years, with a glowing face and eyes like sparks, named Marion Bright (no kidding), composed and delivered a remarkable speech on The 10 Commandments. It stuck so hard I used it through the next 4 decades as an example of putting a new twist in old rope.

She was halfway between rhetorically sensitive and the noble self (see Hart and Burks if you must), leaning hard to the RS. The audience, she guessed (and correctly) didn't like being bossed around, not even by God. So "commandments" by nature would remind us all of submission, rather than the much more deliciously poetic "choice." One chooses to do things much more willingly, perhaps, when they are presented as suggestions.

Ergo, she converted the 10 Commandments. Marion Bright took each of the ten "shalt nots" and turned it into a "try this." (This was long before that schmalz: "Everything .... I Learned in Kindergarten...").

No, she didn't jump right into it, she introduced the idea of turning pushy warnings into positive suggestions slowly, Marionly. She said she'd wished God had called them "The 10 Suggestions," but she figured he knew what he was doing. There is nothing casual about a burning bush.

So, what SHE was doing was making 10 suggestions.

Instead of "thou shalt not steal" MB hit us with, "Keep your hands on your own stuff."

To replace "Thou shalt not kill," she gave us, "Live and let live."

Covet your own spouse.

Covet what you've got.

Admire (so different from envy)

And so on.

Brilliant if the aim is to get people to think about how to live. And she did.

Other speeches were shorter, but still memorable:

- The student who discombobulated the competition right out of the gate in a debate on the 10 Commandments being posted in public buildings (hey, this was 25 years after Marion) by stacking 10 bibles up and saying, "each one of these says something different and I'm still not able to find a numbered list anywhere...so, *which* 10 commandments are the opposition referring to?
- the student who won the "Quarters" speech* by claiming a high vet bill as he'd been playing frisbee with his pet flagella and it broke its tail.
- Ways to Save Money in the Bathroom (lingered on shaving a bit too long)
- The 17 year old who was the primary care-er for her Alzheimer's-stricken aunt,

on how even though she knew it was hopeless to expect her aunt to change or to understand, there were still things she could change in her own communication with her aunt that might help them both feel better.

*described later in this masterpiece

'Tis a shame I don't remember particular speeches in a longer list, but if it means anything I am confident I listened to 30 thousand or more speeches, presentations, and performances and sometimes it was a challenge. Most times it was interesting and way better than teaching from the front. A few well-placed notices and plaudits from my perch amongst the People and on with the show!

This might be one of the popularly perceived soft spots of speech teaching: the time we spend on our arses listening to other people talk. But before ye jump onto that horse, try it for an hour, week, or semester. And provide detailed evaluations that indicate you were conscious during each of the talks and in addition read the supporting documentation. I know, it ain't ditch diggin'. But it ain't easy neither, even after one becomes quick at it.

The most impressive professor of speech I knew in the area of written responses was SIU-Carbondale's R. Paul Hibbs...

July 21, 2020

Before I describe RP Hibbs' style, 'tis time to comment a bit more on current conditions. If Aristotle was right, "you learn to do what you do." I think a more accurate translation goes, "That which you would learn to do, learn by doing." One can read Stanislavsky til one's face blues over like a gun, but until one acts on a stage, rendering a script written by another's hand, in front of an audience of strangers, Stanny don't mean shit. He don't mean that much even after ones does all of the above. "The Creature." Come on.

Today's crises (the whole besotted stack of them, tare weight: infinity) set a background for any form of artistic expression. Crisis inspires art, surely. Look and listen to all of the greatness created during World Wars and other

158

distractions. Mayhem can breed creativity. That has been true through the various (now petty-seeming) crises of my own life. Writing, songwriting, performing, speaking to groups or to an Other--all of this was palliative and therapeutic, and (one hopes) served to freeze aesthetic moments like photographs on beaches.

For some reason, since March 11, I've barely picked up a guitar. Somehow singing seems silly now. How can this be? Was it all tied up with teaching, and now that I'm retired the essential fuel for staying musically loose is gone? Or, is it the Rona, whose tenacious ubiquity and unnerving ambiguity (see Holmes on definitions in *The Copper Beeches*) has this disease, which has not yet touched close to family, committing a larceny of the soul?

What the writer gets past in order to write despite how silly writing is, the musician must also get past. Though the thickly poetic nature of music can make it seem even more frivolous on the surface, compared to all of this really important pecking at keys. Fuck it. I will play again. Just not sure when.

You ain't a musician if you're not playing. And not a singer if you are not singing.

For now I pretend to be a writer, while writing. It's a start.

The teacher also has some barriers to get past:

Are the humanities practical?

Does any of this mean anything anyway?

Who the ____ said Frost was good (or not good)?

If half of the students listen half the time, and the other half half-listens half the time and part of the whole doesn't listen at all, then why talk? Yes, yes, yes, teachers do more than talk...

At my best I was offering two valuable things:

1. A good question attached to a willing ear. and

2. Assignments with useful comments afterward.

Both of those can be engaged whether one is teaching poetry or articulatory phonetics, though there is less delicious ambiguity (a la Hopper) in phonetics.

Before launching off on certain assignments and their observed effects on students in the main, Southern Illinois' R Paul Hibbs deserves praise because he accomplished the second half of the second thing listed above with a style that fit him and the willing students perfectly.

Hibbs taught public speaking, also called public address (a much better name because it includes an audience), so students spent a fair bit of time up front with RP in the rows as an audience member. He took along to his wee desk among the horde just a slender pen and a 3x5 pad of unlined paper. He always seemed, when one dared look toward the teacher while being evaluated on presentation, to be listening. Eyes up, face relaxed, steady, kind. Not the least hint of effort, yet attentive. A model audience member.

His 50 years teaching and coaching speech surely had him attending to many tens of thousands of addresses. So far, maybe you are saying all that's nice but none of that seems remarkable.

Hibbs returned detailed feedback in two forms: his tight, abundant marginalia shared on the speech outline, with suggestions on both form and content aplenty, and the most remarkable little sheet of paper with line after line of perfectly handwritten notes on the speech itself--the kind of details known only to one who had *been there, listening.* The paper was remarkable either way, whether he'd written it during the speech (it appeared so given its chronological character), or afterward (in which case he had an audiographic memory.) That he would, after so many decades listening to students think out loud, care enough to make such carefully written, focused, respectful notes--well, a feller could just get choked up thinking about it. He'd been doing it so long he was bent over from midback to the top of his neck, upon which perched his gravity-defying head, a good head of 77 year old hair staying strong. And he always wore a suit that matched his shoes, with cufflinks enstoned with the same faux gem that graced the front strap on his footoggery. Pure style, no fluff. Like Ibsen, but a semi-retired public speaking teacher in 1978 in Carbondale, IL.

What does any of this have to do with my teaching? At my best, in those years I was giving it the full hell, I did not fill out evaluation forms and "rubrics" that had been converted into scorecards. I scratched nearly inscrutable notes during speeches and later typed letters and stapled them to marked up outlines, just like Hibbs, but without the pleasant and mystically generated handwritten flair. I met a student from that era, who had attended Hampton Institute while I was there, as she visited MSU with a speech team. Crystal Rae Coel (then a college professor and now an Associate Dean) remembered me and the letters about her speeches 15 years after. A little thing like that makes the burned up typewriter ribbons and flat ass all seem worth it.

Wrap all this up to say, even though it is #2 above (and comparable to the other #2 in fragrance at times), providing commentary and feedback on a student's work is the most valuable and valued thing a professor can do.

OK, the most valuable thing that *I* did. You decide for yourself.

Assignments include "exercises" and homework. Between the two, one could study the impact of the in-class exercises, and a couple of them were worth doing over and over, despite the occasional annoyance of some students who either got the point rather too quickly or never got it at all. "The Uncritical Inference Test" in its various forms was a good one. Also, the guessing game what another person might find offensive in language and also what they might guess you might find offensive. Then there is the Quarters Speech.

Side note: yes I stole all of these exercises from people who stole them from people who stole them, like folk songs.

Who Gets The Quarters?

Simple but effective in motivating students to the degree they need, want, or like money. If nearly every one of the 25 students brings in a quarter, that's more than $6, and if the teacher sweetens it a bit, it can hit $10 or more, a tidy sum for a one minute speech.

Each student who plays uses their minute. Those that opt out prove vividly that staying silent can at times lead to losses of financial opportunity. The topic? "Why I Need The Quarters More Than Anyone Else Speaking Today." An applause meter (old tape recorder works well, or an audiometer app), measuring intensity and duration (correcting for clacks supporting their pals.) Your choice if you wish to prohibit socialist promises like, "Give me the money and I will redistribute it to the class based on need..." Yes, people try that. This speech exercise is a gas, sometimes very serious. Most parley into some form of hyperbole (e.g., the aforementioned broken flagella) but on occasion a student truly in need expresses it in moving terms and tones and gets the $ hands down, or hands clapping, as it were.

I used to do an exercise during which each student had to speak for 30 seconds, giving a steady talk on whatever makes them mad. The audience is tasked with heckling the speakers into losing their places or fleeing the scene. Normally quiet, well mannered students turn into an excellent, highly vocal mob. Speakers catch the energy and begin to get drawn into various skirmishes. Audience yells, "Get to the point!" and the speaker points and says, "You're rude, now let me finish." Or various forms of "bugger off." Better speakers simply forge ahead, occasionally amused by the heckling.

Unfortunately, today the tender sensibilities of current students would likely render this exercise "hate speech" even in jest. Tender teachers, too, for that matter.
"Twas a fiery forge, but a grand one that made strong swords." (Jane Francis)

I remember the final time I ran that exercise, a prof from a neighboring classroom stuck her head in the room and used her eyes in splendid glare to signal we'd best be done. And we were. She works for state government now.

The aforementioned Uncritical Inference Test helped students to expand the True/ False dichotomy. A short, 4 line story was followed by 18 True False questions. But a third option was introduced to T and F: the question mark. One could choose T, F or ?. What I learned from this is that T and F are actually Siamese twins. Both are states of certainty. True, the story says so unequivocally. False, the story contradicts unequivocally. The actual distinct state of (un)certainty was marked by the ? It meant, "I know I don't know for sure, for there are provisional meanings here..." in other words, a portion-al knowing that made a firmer decision (T or F) impossible to make with confidence *based on the story*. To me, this was useful training to become a juror, a debater, an advocate, and a rhetorician. Refry the cliche, "To know you do not know, this is wisdom." (Confucius?) Students first worked alone, then with a partner, then the entire group, and along the way 95-100% of the participants changed at least one answer, and most often from a wrong one to a right one. Among the dozens of exercises run through the decades, this one seemed most practically valuable. Not just because it was good prep to be a juror (and a good excuse to talk about that duty and what we all would hope our jurors be able to do...), the UIT was a chance to see that when we work alone we can make errors which are easily detected and corrected by teaming up and communicating with others.

Error-detection.

Correction.

Growth.

Amen.

The Changing Dread

People dread public speaking, as the legend goes (though we have established they do not choose death when given the choice). People report dreading Public Speaking classes and classes that require it. I learned two things in relation to those predilections: 1) reality TV and social media have reduced reticence, particularly concerning first-person narration and biography (whereby today nearly everything becomes biographical), and 2) if you give people only a *very* brief time to make their point, most of the time they fill all of the time and still have something to say. That's a sly goose to get them to want to do it again.

Debaters know the feeling, but it's got general application, too.

A question well framed is worth an hour of lecture, depending on the topic. A bunch of rhetorical questions and bad Socratism all lined up to lead the audience to mouth what the lecturer would have said anyway, this is abuse of method and should be punishable by forced reading the entirety of *The Quarterly Journal of Speech.*

As I try to recall the things I did a lot that seemed to be worthwhile and not simply "content," (ugh), many days for many years I would have a quotable quote on the board. Some of my favorites:

"Gravity is a drag."

"Is a poet simply a lost typist?"
and

"Compose or decompose."
All by the magnificent Jane Francis.
and

"Creativity is contagious," (for decades I believed was an original thought) of William Sherman Minor*, was perhaps not his own expression. The other night I was watching a documentary on the Bonneville Salt flats and Abner___. There on the back of his speeding car in the 1950's, painted where the spare tire cover would hang, "Creativity is contagious."

Dr. Minor was good about attributions, so maybe Ab was quoting *him.*

William Sherman Minor (1900-1991) quoted many other persons and thus provided quotes I used often:

"Curiosity trumps certainty."

as its inverse is also true, I added:
"Certainty trumps curiosity."
These are important points in a range of communication classes. Can't think of one where they are not.
I also liked to draw this on the board,

N
W   E
S

particularly in classes having to do with public communication, and ask students what was happening in the 4 directions, often adding up and down (space and the subterranean/marine). Why? Speech class goes so much better when there is something to talk about.

This is, purported by someone I've forgotten, the source of the word NEWS.

Having students read aloud in class under duress used to be more common as so many classes I taught were mainly performance-based. But toward the end, when courses became more cranial, reading aloud became a diverting oddity.

A typical class would, after the song, move right to an inquiry: "who will read from our two works today?" The dictionary was one, the other either Kramer's *Book of Curiosities* (outdated but good even when wrong) or Panati's *Extraordinary Origins of Everyday Things*. The latter provided hundreds of examples of such ordinary things as the toilet, silly putty, eyeglasses, and Teflon and accidentally along the way illustrated how important curiosity, questioning, observation, and a willingness to fuck around led to useful inventions. Oh, and Vaseline.

Making a class portion appear to be a delaying tactic to avoid starting class is a dastardly fine thing to do. Thus were my intros, which could last anywhere from 3 minutes to most of the period.

July 23, 2020

An elementary school teacher once spoke eloquently to me about how touch has been redefined over the last 20 years. Because of the prevalence of reports about sexual abuse of children and women (almost never about men...), sensitivity and attention to ALL forms of touch ensued. Tossing aside its therapeutic and palliative qualities, touch was redefined by authorities as fundamentally sexual. Because touch *could* be sexual, it therefore was assumed to *be* sexual, depending on the perverted predispositions of the toucher and/or the observer. Soon, observers became as perverted as the perverts, because they saw sexual touch everywhere. Any time an adult touched a child, then, it was either a manifestation or a potential precursor to abuse. Solution? Ban touch.

Teachers were ordered never to touch their students. If a student needed touching (medical, discipline, etc.) escort them to the appropriate office, wherein, under witness, an authorized adult will determine what or if touching was needed and whom might dispense said touching.

This was instituted for everyone's "safety." Safety, the new God. Safety, what all of us deserve but none of us really ever have. Nature has been trying to take each of us out since day 1. The no-touchers strive to take this starting place and to disallow everything that might worsen an already bad predicament. You v. nature. A mismatch. Rigged. But one way to fight the horror is to prevent its furtherance.

So, all bicycle riders should wear helmets because some have accidents. And all children should be protected from adult touch (and the touch of one another) because some pervy adults (and kids) commit crimes.

All that as background, this elementary teacher had had enough. A 30-year veteran, she'd never been told such foolishness about touching students during the early part of her career; never crossed her mind. The recent dicta upset her for several reasons, but her defiance was singular: "If a first grader runs up to me and needs a hug, whether they've fallen down or are just saying good morning or goodbye, dammit I am going to hug them back. The board can go ahead and fire me. Or try to."

I believe they'd have messed with the wrong teacher.

And by "they" I mean all the good-hearted, well-intentioned, road-to-hell-pavers trying to make all kids "safe" all the time.

Oh my, now even adults are making claims based on their plummeting sense of safety. College students (adults for the most part and the legal part), some of them older than I, can and do now claim their safety is threatened by viewpoints they find unacceptable. This is easily documented, but I'd rather get to what I think about it:

I've not really run into complaints at MSU based on this "safety" or "safe space" issue, but MSU has just recently developed an ambitious "inclusion" program, a feature of which is a "bias reporting process" wherein anonymous complaints can be posted ("every one of which will be investigated") when someone's safety is claimed to have been threatened. This includes feelings of being unsafe. It could happen anywhere, any time. NOT having run into this between 1991 and 2020 was nice, but I was always waiting for it and did get a tug of it now and then.

No, we ought not blame students for this. They appear to have been well-schooled in the language of anxiety. In the 20th century it was called "angst" and was practiced by people with dark clothes, a love of Camus and too much spare time. Now it is "anxiety" and is the engine for multi-billion dollar industries that serve to treat or cure it. Oh, and define it.

The number of students freely reporting "anxiety" and taking days for mental health has gone from just about 0.1% to I'd rather not say.

No, they are not to blame. "You learn to do what you do," as Ari said.

Perhaps the world has changed into a place that manufactures anxiety with facility, for a host of reasons and through natural processes. Yet for a teacher, working across 4 decades during which (last 5 months aside) all kinds of scary shit went down, the recent levels of anxiety that were built up from say 1999 forward may or may not be entirely attributable to actual worsening conditions.

Not to wander too far off the point here: teaching. The river of students that flow before one over the terms and years is highly variable, and polluted. Polluted by:

1. things taught to them as factual that are not

2. random rules and policies that are backward

3. rituals

4. traditions

5. medicines

Hate me if you want to, but we've got to admit that the overmedication of our children (and ourselves?) is a fact, a practice that must have effects as that is exactly what it is designed to do. "Hyperactivity" is something we ought to have asked Marie Curie, Edison, Twain, or

DaVinci, Millay or Keller about. It's a nasty name for what at times is a golden thing. Medication designed to tamp down behavior that is disfavored because it disrupts the factory-education system is tamping down the things that come with excitement: energy, drive, uncontrollable urges to make, to build, to tear down and rebuild.

Cure one ill, sow another.

This was already a problem in the 1990's and no telling how much bigger it has gotten. Folks who were dosed for their own good who are now having children would not find anything peculiar about dosing in the main.

For teachers, responding to higher sensitivity means imagining oneself as they might be now, unused to certain levels of energy, threatened by refutation, easily harmed by mere contradiction or even a follow up question. I have seen these things develop and become more prominent. An advantage to being a speech teacher is that one hears in voices the changing melody of "civility." That is because our materiel is voice and body. But even in debate class (of all places) in 2020 a more delicate approach seemed apropos compared to 2000.

Maybe it was the towers coming down that shook everyone up. No, most of my students in 2020 were but ova and flagella back then. Huh.

I think there is a point here that has to do with teaching: learning is uncomfortable. By nature. It is like shedding a skin, or growth pains, or the knitting of a broken bone. We professors do not need to do things to make it hurt more than it does by nature. But to try to reform, mold, control, and mollify it into something that is never uncomfortable, scary, even risky...sorry, that's to kill it. After that, education can be equated with "content delivery" over which the receiver has total discretion and editorial control.

New motto for higher ed: As long as what you are teaching, and how, and what you are asking of them, doesn't make anyone too "uncomfortable," OK, then. YOU may proceed.

But lard bless MSU, things never got too bad in my classes. I think doing my best Larry B___ rendition of "Oklahoma Hills," tended to smoke the hive a bit. Once a white student did say something about his own white privilege during a discussion. He went unchallenged, even from the people in the room who were the first to get out of the holler from their family and on to a campus or who had a habit of eating that could not always be exercised. Pin drop. Now *that* is privilege.

A more pronounced case of anxiety living just under the crust happened in a class where the aforementioned Carl Albright, 85 year old bent over terror who claimed to be a bodyguard for L Ron Hubbard, joined me and a couple of other students in some kind of discussion over something that was energizing. The instant things began to get louder than polite conversation would dictate (but free of ire, more like the best moments of baseball) the male student said, as if to children (during a tornado) "Hey hey hey hey! Calm down, you guys. There is no need to yell," his voice lightly laced with quavering perturbation. I guess that is a primary communication symptom of high anxiety (which of course there really are lots of reasons for): hearing yelling where there is no yelling.

Sometimes this oversensitivity is a function of how a student's home life proceeded. Certain families simply never raised their voices. For others, any form of raised voice is paradigmatic with every other raised voice, which means a species of anger or pending violence. And in 2020, the result of years of efforts by morons, speaking itself is equated with violence. Loud or energetic speaking motivated by vigor and the *élan vital**, well, that's just wrong. Someone might not feel "safe." I was happy to see that more than half the room that moment didn't know what the heck he was worried about, as none of the interlocutors did either. Tilted heads, odd looks, but pure recognition by me that the broader context of conversation had

shifted, and people were more and more on the lookout for infractions against "safety."
_{*thank you, Henri Bergson.}

Back to touching...

The boldness of that elementary teacher was inspiring because I had so long ago resigned myself to never touching or being touched when students and colleagues were involved. Handshakes, OK, if you must. But taps, raps, arm touches, hugs? No. Not even when someone is weeping or getting ready to pass out. Let the floor stop them. Sad. But 'tis something one can practice most of the time, until a student comes along that is a hugger. Just that, nothing more. No sex. No allure. Nothing pervy or nasty or unrequited from childhood. Just a hugger.

What is a straight white man to do? Give in, godammit. Hug back; keep it grandfatherly, and try not to blush.

I suppose you could claim that such behavior is "unsafe." And you would be right, but not because hugs are scientifically known to be harmful. Quite the opposite in fact. Still, a hug is so ambiguous that minds fascinated by perversion are wont to perceive hugging as perverted. A student hugging a professor is a display so easily understood as sexual that it might be enough to render one unsafe. Why handshakes are not perceived this way is beyond me. Hands, palms and fingers are much more sexually intimate than the average hug.

Oh there are all sorts of things that used to be innocent but are now grounds for suspicion, like being a priest, or

1. office doors (best just to take them off the hinges entirely)

2. covered windows (what are you hiding?)

3. any form of gaze (equals ogling)

So concerned about being accused, I would rarely shut the door to my office when I was alone in there, for fear I might end up harassing myself (which I did on several occasions; whereupon I accessed mediation instead of filing formal charges.)

July 25, 2020

If you are still reading it is because you managed to get by my earlier example of correcting the facts on Michael Brown's tragic shooting without condemning me as a nutjob right winger. If I am one, I am in good company with others who conceded the officer's lack of guilt (Obama, Holder, the locals on the Ferguson case grand jury, esteemed playwrights, etc.). You could be forgiven for either choice: to condemn or to continue reading, or both. Racism, bigotry, and radicalism had nothing to do with my choice to speak up and correct the story of Michael Brown, though Dr. Minor might say radicalism did have something to do with it since the radical "seeks the root." In any such case where a professor corrects a student, or a colleague, or is correctly corrected by them, Henry Nelson Wieman's reflection pertains. According to Dr. Minor, old Wieman was challenged when his wee son hopped on his lap and asked him, "Who is Jesus?" Pausing to think (not a bad idea), Wieman said to himself, "What can I teach him that he won't have to unlearn later?"

That is what moved me to correct the student about Hands Up Don't Shoot. And that is what motivates the following exemplars, sad as they may be.

If I had let that gentleman, and the class, continue to wallow in misinformation, I would have been perpetuating their later downfall. They would have to, possibly at great cost, unlearn what they had been taught or led to believe. Leading someone to some belief often involves leading away from some, too.

Granting that students make things up, one watches for corroboration or some kind of verification when outrageous stories are told.

One day at the start of a class close to a major election, I asked,

"Are you talking politics in your other classes?"

Brief pause; bold student speaks up,

"Yes, just the other day we were told by Prof G__ that if we voted Republican we were stupid."

That on its face would be hard to believe. For what professor in their right mind would say such a thing about either major party? Others corroborated with nods and comments. This tale was consistent with similar such stories from past election seasons (and when isn't it election season in the US?)

Another professor who loudly shared party affiliation with the aforementioned Prof G__ was described by students as so punitive to wrong student politics that, as one woman remarked, "It is better to hide your own ideas and write papers for her that match her ideology." This was "the way to get an A from Professor T__."

To myself I said, "this cannot be true," but when such tales are told across years, one begins to think the students are being taught something they will have to unlearn later. The ends justify the means, to such persons harassing students this way, whom I hesitate to call professors.

In Conflict & Communication, close descriptions of incidents of observable conflict were shared profusely. Conflict in communication is one area of storytelling that provides a cauldron of tales. A male MSU student reported that he was entering Rader Hall, home to programs in humanities such as Sociology, Criminology, Gender Studies (formerly Women's Studies), Geography, and the Dean's Office. Before he got to the door he observed that it was being held open for the heavily-laden woman who was entering in front of him. According to the story, she stopped and excoriated a male student who was holding the door open for her. She was carrying things, and spoke firmly with loud, sharp-edged accusations of sexism, misogyny, etc. The entire recipe of toxic masculinity.

He holding the door appeared to be surprised, according to the report.

The challenge for the conflict class was delicious: how to reckon his value of doorholding with her value of never having a door held for her or any woman? Consider for a moment what that irate professor (or staffer or admin) was "teaching" at that moment. Praise aside for creating such a juicy example for my class, this may not have been productive.

Women who are sick of being treated as if they are frail may be so fed up that the woman's forceful language and tone seem entirely justified, reflective of long-tempered, deep tines of anger. The question is, do most people live in that paradigm?

Hers: males holding doors is an iteration of detested chivalry.

His: people in front hold doors for people behind, regardless of the shape of their skin.

She certainly had a point: one *could* see such apparently chivalrous behavior as profane in many paradigms. But was her's the best way to make that point?

182

What would you do?

Such a juicy and delicious example. I wonder if it's true.

Discussions that developed in class about the "incident" nearly always moved quickly to the behavior of door-opening itself. Why do it? (Because it's nice, helpful, courteous, and a practical way to keep things flowing and to avoid hitting people in the face with doors.) For whom to do it? (Everyone. Period.) Though one student did admit that an auxiliary function might be so the holder can check out the entrant's ass.

The only place where *I* can see prolonged door-holding as a problem is in an elevator.

Alert: the next section is even more pedantic than usual, so skip ahead if language and how it is spoken bothers you.

And remember: I didn't invent English.

Many if not most students, particularly those schooled in formal reading, have been taught English words that do not exist or pronunciations that are not consistent with the lexicon and traditional practice. To wit: *the* and *a.*

July 27, 2020   *THE and A*

Probably best to stick here to stories that I know are true, or at least of which I have had some direct observations. The story of last entry concerning the contentious opening of a door was corroborated, and besides it is the kernel of the question that even a fiction would raise: why is it that the symbolic paradigm selected is so often the most negative one (regarding motive)?

Then there are just stupid, yet traditional mistakes that I probably spent too much time trying to correct. This was not style, or dialect, or accent. This was English ferchrissakes. And, duly noted, I did not invent it. As a teacher I had a duty to point out its diminution and to try not to let anything that might need to be unlearned later slip by me.

You can call a trunk a boot and I'm fine. You can call a package a parcel, for that matter.

184

But when you mispronounce "a" and "the" *when you're inviting feedback* from me *on your speech*, then you're gonna hear some comments.

Need I insult the reader by reviewing the rules? If you know them, a satisfying review that verifies you are not the only person who knows them will be your reward for reading on. If you do not know the rules, you can get your back up and deny thricefold, or you can get on board. Your choice.

THE is pronounced "thuh" when the next *sound* is a consonant sound. Not simply a consonant--a consonant *sound*. Saying the word for the "M" (a consonant) of MSU, for example, does not begin with a consonant sound. The name of the letter M is pronounced "em." Thus, we say THEE MSU, not THUH MSU. Etc.

"A" is not an article in English when pronounced [e] as in IPA and Spanish. We say [e] when naming the letter A, or stating a grade A or a top quality measurement. But we should say "uh" (aka the schwa or short U) when the letter functions as a word. There is no such article as [e]. Before a vowel sound we say "an." Don't blame me I didn't invent this mess.

The above two common errors, the explanation in every case has been that teachers taught students that when they are reading aloud formally they are to say THEE for "the" and [e] as in "bait" for "a" each time, regardless of context.

Fucking teachers.

Work your way back to the first one who taught this bullshit and apply the description above.

My fervent yet measured clarification of this rule seemed most of the time to fall on rocky ground. And the tender seeds of my cultural preservation were tread upon by the heavy foot of error's infamous momentum.

This evening I really wanted to forget the rioting, burning, looting, clashing, shooting, bombing, artillery and utter symbolic foolishness and madness ablend in our the cities and afield on this day. Just to forget and to watch *Casino* or something. But I had to get that thing about THEE and [e] as in bait off my chest.

I feel better now, thanks.

If I am not going to write about anything much tonight I ought at least to write about what I hope to write about:

Smoking in class

Parties

The Subject

The library

Conferences with students

The Magic 168

Memorable colleagues and things they said

The places I have taught as places to live
Small spaces
The hellish ease of the "academy"
Presidents
Remembering Cynthia Martin (9.11)
Statues and building texts
Blue collar among funny clothing
Thank you's
Fuck you's
The Universal Theory
    Might even get to some of the above some
day. Fear not, surely areas of it are already too
murky...

July 28, 2020

Talk of a vaccine entering Stage III trials today. Yeah. I know. Of course it would be done already if Trump wasn't so orange.

Last entry was about common errors against which students needed vaccination: silly rules of pronunciation intended to signal refinement when really what they signaled was someone trying to signal refinement (and failing.)

Today I first consider the challenges and rewards of remembering students' names. Without question, the student who spoke often or at all had a much higher chance of a name being remembered. I know that it mattered to them every time I managed to recall their names a day, week, month, year or decade (or 2) after meeting them. I honestly did remember students much more than I did their names.

Faces, sounds, aspects, features, even speeches they gave. And sometimes their names...
Except for one name I'll never forget even if I hit my head.

In 2009 or so during a period on campus when people might be expected to have returned to visit (either Homecoming or some such), I happened to be walking up near Eagle Lake, and topped the dam where there were benches, very often occupied. The bench nearest the path to the dam top was occupied by 3 people this pleasant evening. An older woman and two younger. Their comportment immediately suggested family to me, and as usual I was going to slip by and walk down by the spillway at the other end of the bank.

"Dr. Modaff!" I heard a one of the younger voices call. The sound was not one of "You owe me money!" but rather more a melody of surprise and glee.

I heard the mother or the sister whisper, "...he will never remember you."

The woman who called my name stood and moved toward me as I turned toward the bench, pretending not to have noticed them until then.

"Hello--"

"--my mother thinks you won't remember me. Is she right?"

I did not need to look away, search my skull, or in any way pause to remember,

"Cynthia Martin."

She nearly hopped off the dam, giving her mom one of those looks that was good natured but savored victory.

"Yes, I remember you, "I said. "You suffered through Speech For Teachers and Oral Interp years ago."

"That's right." We chatted a bit about the class and then her mother expressed amazement at my memory.

"Well," I admitted, "'Tis not only that your daughter was extraordinary in classes. Cynthia also is stuck in my memory for another reason."

Their looks were request enough to continue.

"Cynthia told me about the 9/11 attacks just moments after they happened. Outside on the courtyard stairs of the Combs Building. She came up, excited but not happy. 'We've been attacked...' she said."

I looked at Cynthia. Her family may not as well have been there for a moment.

"I will never forget it." I said.

And she nodded, "I remember."

That reframed the memory, from one of joyful good luck to a lesson on how things get burned into the dendrites of the mind. Did that diminish or did it enhance whatever significance my recalling her name might have had?

When you've had somewhere between 8 and 9 thousand students (lost count long ago), remembering every name is going to be a challenge. And since you might encounter only a fraction of a percent of them ever again, knowing which names to remember would also be impossible. So when I did encounter a student of mine (sometimes 20 years later or more) and did recall the name, the blending of good fortune was almost always something to behold.

Time came when I was teaching the children of my former students. Happened again last term, my last term. I pretended not to notice.

Using the phrase "last term" reminds me that my language will need to be reformed, as I am an Eskimo who has moved to a rainforest. Not a complaint, but an observation. The language of belonging to a school, which I have used since 1964 as student and teacher, is hard to strip away cleanly and suddenly, even though that is how retirement happens. Now, *all* of my students are former students. That has not been true before. We shall see how fate tosses new opportunities to recall names.

A name I cannot recall is that of the SIU bodybuilder who seemed to me to be making up for his lack of altitude and aptitude with a growth of muscular girth, mostly above the waist. An impressive set of gym-fed muscles left a little room for his backpack. Anyhow, I think his steroids were either working too well or not well enough one evening after class when he offered, upon learning of his likely grade, to "break one or both of "my legs. I took him only half seriously and so moved only one leg back. There were witnesses, so he rethought his plan.

I remember the first name of a student who corrected my Spanish dialect pedantry once (Brian C__) and who came back two and a half years later to apologize (right before asking me for a favor.) I was amazed he remembered it as I did. An obscure but relevant point about [b] and [v] overlapping or some shit. He wasn't apologizing for being wrong, only that I was right.

Which reminds me of something I said quite often to classes across the decades, not knowing whether it is an original observation (as with so many I've made over the years) concerning correcting the everyday diction or articulation of others: "If I know how to correctly correct you, then I know what you meant in the first place." That is, in polite conversation (*viz*. not in class), correcting someone when they say "whelp" instead of "welt" is just plain rude. I knew what you meant, unless context made it possible you had puppies lounging on your forearm.

So, why correct you? During speech class this polite rule is suspended, just as writing teachers suspend the rules of polite reading in order to help their students improve. Outside of classes, though, 'tis rude and uncalled for unless the Other has requested your sage guidance on their speech patterns.

Doubtful.

A student at Hampton once told me during class that my fly was open. I adjusted the device ASAP but then turned to the room and said, "I'd say thank you but first wonder why it took thirty minutes for anyone to say something." Laughter quickly obscured the need for explanation.

I once had a grad student, MA level, express concern, "I had no idea graduate school involved so much READING!" It helped but little when I said, "If you don't read all of these articles, who will?"

I've had students say that I was the best prof they'd had (so far). Most others did not say that. RateMyProfessors says I can be moody. What kind of shit is that? Now I *am* mad.

Speaking of Rate My Professors.com, which is a complete gas and full of the same, an example of long-lasting impact became evident when, 25 years after my departure from Alfred University, an AU student posted comments about my Voice and Articulation class. And not entirely good. No appetite for bluntness, I guess. The content is not the oddity--the lateness of the posting is. How flattering to be remembered for *anything* after 25 years.

Maybe I have so much trouble remembering names because I made it a point to not get close to my students as a rule. Sounds weird, I suppose. But all of the decades of burgeoning cautions about privacy, intimacy, and harassment led me to keep a distance. That distance could easily be traversed by any student who truly needed something, of course. Otherwise I avoided students by living in a bubble of anonymity and mystery to students, like the Green Hornet.

Except for one. Allison Forman. And I am married to her now.

See what happens?

A tribute to the success of my 'pretending not to notice' campaign for students was that my spouse-to-be had no idea I thought she was the most beautiful woman I'd ever seen. Two classes came and went with no such inklings... She just thought I was strange in a good way and was convinced of it when I stopped teaching once to adjust my shoe laces.

Our 20th anniversary is next year. She has exemplary taste.

I wasn't exactly fending off offers, to be sure. My professional bubble was super effective in obviating what slew of attempts might otherwise have come from students of all kinds. Sometimes the professor is the first person who ever really listened to them, or spoke to them as an adult. That can be appealing. One wants that sort of appeal, but wants also for it to stop right there.

A few years after coming to MSU I had a student in my first morning class who was from Colorado, possessing all of the natural beauty of that fine state, but in a lopped off sort of way that suggested a future career in kickboxing. Her morningly visits became a regular thing and at times she sat with nothing to say and didn't seem to mind at all--a very bad sign to someone tending a bubble. Without planning, though, a solution inserted itself into the flow. One morning I was minutes away from starting the first class, pecking something out on the computer, which stood tall enough for me to stand, over near the window. The door was 10 feet to my left, so unless I tended to the periphery, people could arrive unnoticed. Well, Colorado did just that, and caught me picking my nose in a most unambiguous way. How unfortunate in the grand scheme to be caught one knuckle up. But alas and aha, she never did come to visit again and sit quietly through silences. The bubble preserved, by a booger!

July 31, 2020---*The Necessary Evil of the Illusion of Arbitrariness*

Is interaction with a purpose manipulation? If so, all rhetoric is manipulation. That can't be right. Lots of good things would stop without rhetoric. All enticement, all allure (of the lexical kind), art itself.

The title of this entry was written a year ago, in a different world. On a different world. But you couldn't tell it by looking at nature. Nature has itself become easier and creatures and atmospheres have improved in their health. But hey let's not get distracted from The Mission: teaching.

When a teacher has done a thing, any rhetorical thing, over and over thousands of times across classes and terms and years and decades, it must still somehow appear and sound new to the students of the moment. This is an unintentional rhetorical predicament: (a) have a plan, and (b) behave as if what is happening is unplanned (and thus novel, fresh, desirable).

One can sometimes see and hear the terminus of one's argument beginning to form in the minds and out of the mouths of the students. One need not say, "yah, this be dialectic..." for them to learn from a good example (like the door holding incident) that two legitimate yet competing values can coexist in the same mind at once. Horse to water? Not that simple. Just even try to Machiavelli them to a conclusion and the knife-minded ones will object just because.

This would be the place, dear reader, where you might expect the author to launch an exemplar or two, wot? Why not, you say, prove that this rhetorical predicament is real by describing what happened when it happened?

All I can say is that I know it began to happen in the last ten years of teaching, wherein a stable set of courses and a constant flow of repetition of planned moments got me thinking, "here this is again--happening."

Just as if it had been planned.

This is the potentially evil rhetoric that, in the hands of a capable but soul-free operator, can lead to masses of ignorant populations
or
lots of smarter people.

Is this nothing more than a quasi-poetic ode to the enthymeme?

I leave it to you to answer that.

***

Note: a speech teacher must ever tell oneself that even though one has heard dozens of speeches on smoking and its dangers, one has not heard THIS speech on the topic.

Students took some interesting angles on speeches that might have been censored in other prof's sections of the class. No censorship in my classes, ever, as I recall. The only thing that was censored was censorious speech. The reward was that at speech # 400 on a topic someone does something different with it--but not just different; different and better. To wit:

Dozens upon dozens of speeches on abortion, as you can imagine, spilt through the air and into my brain holes as I sat attentively watching while striving to scrawl something I'd be able to read later. Most who chose the topic chose to object to the right to choose, taking every version of that tune one could whistle and developing it with varying levels of graphicality. One speaker stood out. One speaker dared to move beyond the legal question--not to dismiss it, but to set it aside so "we could talk."

The speaker was a female, very well-prepared, one who had not spoken much during classes yet always did so competently when addressing the room from the front. She began quietly, letting us know that where she stood on the issue of abortion, or even where the supreme court stood, was of no concern during her talk today. She wanted to talk to us about the choice we had, not the legality of it.

The speech, framed in this way--pro-choice entirely in the most fundamental way--allowed her to emphasize that whether the government is involved or not, the choice to end a pregnancy was a woman's choice. This pro life speaker was establishing a set of common values, centered on choice, to make her persuasive claim: you *should* treat it as a choice, one of the most important you may ever make. Given that, then, the question of what is right towers before you. That is the far more important question. What will *you* do? She ended. An enthymeme on steroids. Plain, basic, skillful, rhetorically facile because she surrendered to the axiom that people are gonna do whatever the fuck they choose.

But choose they will.

Odd how from among tens of thousands of speeches and presentations, a few linger in detail, others in impression or a recollection of an effect. The word "fuck" brings two cases to mind.

"Is a poet just a lost typist?"

--Jane Francis

August 1, 2020: *Gender and Fuck*

My friend Vaughn Deel over in Hampton used to say he never discriminated against people based on the shape of their skin. A good rule to follow. However, when bodies do get together, all sorts of features become notable and appear to have a communicative function. To wit, the story of two students who, on the same day and within minutes of one another, uttered the word "fuck" in class with quite different results.

The scene: Hampton Institute, circa 1983, speech class. Before the days of playing guitar to open, I would invite someone to read a word and etymology from the dictionary ("our leap into the lexicon"), and then solicit a joke from anyone willing to tell it. Jokes had flowed regularly and nearly always tastefully. Even those that crept toward the naughty did so with due trepidation and furtive yet smiling glances toward the teacher. As if I'd give a fuck.

So we'd been into the joke telling for a while. Hey, it's a speech class. Any time students are making speeches work is being done.

Kathy B___, vivacious in every sense of the word, in appearance and voice, took to the front of the room. In those days we always stood when addressing the group formally. Like the pioneers.

Kathy had a voice that would just as well have come from a 9 year old in half of its timbre. This portended if not naiveté, then innocence. The other half was still light, but sultry, witty, mischievous. And, because she was beautiful, this unusual combination became just another part of her allure, rather than a cartoonish impediment to adulthood. Her composition, then, as mind, body and voice, was rhetorically facile quite before she uttered a word.

Kathy doe-ed to the front of the room, long tight braids flowing from her head, and turned quickly to begin:

"Little Red Riding Hood was walking
through the wood, all red and looking good.
The wolf jumped out from behind a tree and
tried to sweet-talk her:
'I'm gonna *fuck* you Little Red Riding Hood!' he
growled.
(light inhalation from the room)
Lil Red stopped him short, held up her hand in
his face and said,
'No way. You're gonna *eat* me just like the
story says.' "

Uproarious laughter from all corners of the
room. Good humor does not discriminate. A
quick smiling bow and a firefly's dance back to
her seat.

Barely was there time to reflect on the
rhetorical and comedic, dare we say poetic
achievement of slipping the word fuck into class
without creating any sort of moral ripple, when
a young gentleman volunteered to end joke time
with a joke of his own. Why not? Kathy B's
was quick enough to leave time for another.

I cannot remember the gentleman's name,
but I can see his face now, and his look of
expectation. After my own reflection and
analytical criticism of this rhetorical moment
over years while mowing various lawns, I
conclude he thought the fetters were off, that the
rules on language had been suspended.
Suddenly, his hesitance to speak during joke
time due to moral trip lines was gone. Kathy B

had just tossed the f-word AND referred to cunnilingus in the same joke! Hoooeee! Wild West!

Or so he thought.

He forgot that audiences commit attribution errors and bestow the halo effect on speakers unguided by rationality most of the time. People are moved by language AND its delivery. Kathy B had everything going for her: primacy in joke time and in tossing the f-word, a genteel aspect that belied her pornographic intentions, a loving personality that gave her an ethological trustworthiness. The audience let her do as she wished. Alas, the gentleman had none of that going for him: the recency effect is not an advantage in a set of 2; generally quiet so not speaking out of a known vocal repertoire; and (sad to say) his maleness reframed his speech, in that what is indelicate yet hilarious from a lovely young woman is merely boorish from an otherwise unremarkably handsome young man.

Dear reader, you might wonder why a professor committed to NOT noticing how people look would loiter so long on the details of their appearances in that fabled joke time. Remember, I am not explaining why I laughed or did not laugh (fuck is fuck as far as I'm concerned), but rather what the audience of their peers did in reaction.

The gentleman tossed off a joke a few people had not heard and it also involved the word fuck. Immediately it became apparent that the context in which he used it, lacking as it was in Grimm pedigree, was not amusing to the audience. He perhaps had sorely miscalculated that the operative word in KB's joke was "fuck" when actually it was "eat." Rhetorical bungling in his audience analysis, it was. Bungling also in assuming the rules had changed just because a classmate had broken them. Clearly he did not spend much time around beautiful women.

They reacted to his joke with curt, jittery laughter that sounded embarrassed for him rather than amused by him. He slunk back to his desk, confused by a moment that probably still makes him wonder.

Moral? While to me a fuck is a fuck, to audiences a fuck is not a fuck.

It's a semiotic problem. Paradigm warfare, Richard Lanigan, regal semiotician of SIU, might aver if he would allow himself to speak poetically.

I do not recall saying the entire f-word in class until about 1995, when, during a graduate class in communication theory, a current reading examined the function of "examples" as a value in discourse. Making an example of something changes its status, one might say. So, saying the word fuck, for example, could be excused because it was not uttered as an expletive, but an example of one. See?

Fok.

I've been typing without my shoes on and I must say it is nice in a way or two but generally a distraction. All my shoes are wet because the dew is so dang heavy here you could almost drink it.

Things professors said...

The great Dr. Marvin Kleinau of SIU-Carbondale commented just once directly on a worthy point, during a speech he was giving at an Honor's convocation, I believe. "The learning is not in the books," he spoke with a chuckle. And then surprised me, out in the audience, "John Modaff knows that, don't you Modaff?"
I waved sheepishly and nodded, singled out among an audience of hundreds.
Took a while to realize this was not a dismissal of the book, any book. Dr. K was noting that what we *do* with the book, the talk we have around it like a fire we share, *that* is where we learn. A smart and superbly euphonious man, Dr. K.

Along the way other things speakers said stuck with me as fundamental axia that surely guided my teaching a dozen ways and thousands of times. At UT-Austin the famous rhetorician Carroll Arnold had come to speak a guest of the

Department of Speech Communication. In a well-appointed, richly wooded gathering space across the street from the program's digs, Dr. Arnold made some interesting observations that he said were new to him, fresh thinking. That was when he laid down the one line of that speech that stuck with me:

"I would not have thought of these things if you had not asked me to give this speech."

I guess this is what the gang meant when they said "rhetoric is epistemic.

Dr. William Sherman Minor (1900-1991) of SIU-Carbondale, professor of creative communication and the philosophy of creativity, said and jotted on the board many useful things that I repeated or made the basis of units or activities. While he may not have originated any of these thoughts, he was the first person ever to say them in my presence and apply them sensibly to questions of meaning and conduct in communication:

"Creativity is contagious."

"Curiosity trumps certainty."

"Punishment is the crime of all crimes."

"Don't rebel."

"People often swing from rebel to slave."

I think "don't rebel" was his antidote to "don't enslave yourself." He saw them as adjacents but not opposites. The only time he ever said it to me was when I was starting to buck having been assigned to read John

Dewey's *Art As Experience*, a lovely but mortally pedantic examination of how meaning enters life. I didn't know at the time how much Dewey contributed to the downfall of our empire, but that book was damn good if one does not mind ten foot long sentences with none of the panache of Melville.

One of the most helpful quotes that I have ever come across is one attributed to William James. I recall the quotation and the section in which it appeared in *Book of Lists*, wherein was listed things people had said while on nitrous oxide (aka laughing gas.) James was said to have said the following:

"There are no differences but differences of degree between degrees of difference and no difference."*

Reading quickly, one is convinced the gas has scrambled his mind. But this is William James, whose mind scrambled is equal to ten of mine still in the shells.   What could it mean?

It came to mean, for me, that studies in social science using statistics to make claims about what people do, think, feel, or what they intend, will, or might do are to be read with his quote top-of-mind. The articles become much more enjoyable and the charts and tables become less cumbersome. Try it.

*There is some dispute as to the exact wording, but I'm sticking with this.

August 2, 2020

The world is ending right on schedule, just more slowly than required to cause complete panic. That will come.

Meantime, I strive ever harder to recall stories about my teaching "career" that you, an older me or a stranger, might enjoy. That is precisely not the reason to write. Reminder: you are writing this shit down so you don't forget it...no, that's not right. You are writing this shit down now for when you do forget it later. Then, like watching a movie one knows one has seen but remembers naught, the experience can be appreciated in a fresh way. The good wages of amnesia.

Texas, Austin, the feeling of money in hills.
For the time I was there, I never heard anyone
say there was not enough of anything. Surely
deep in the throes of the faculty and staff
political bodies, the insatiable appetite for more
of everything did result in the illusion of
deprivation. But for God's sake, the sidewalks
were works of art, inlaid with dyed semi-smooth
pebbles, in a mosaic that, if ground smooth
would resemble terrazzo. And this was outside.
Grand edifices, sayings of olden wisdom,
hidden courtyards with statues of important
personages and their swords and books. The
tower, the one that no one can look at without
saying the name Whitman at least once. The
library. The librar*ies*. All of them grand and
stuffed full of whatever you might imagine to
read. And while I was not on the faculty there, I
did teach classes in public speaking and
interpersonal communication, topics of which I
knew sore little but did not know I did not
know. Thus I say, with pride, that I taught at the
University of Texas. I look with shock now at
the responsibility laid upon us Teaching
Assistants, just 3 months as we were from
graduating college the first time. But hail
circumstance: their demand invited my supply.

Southern Illinois, Carbondale. Not Texas,
but lovely in its own way. Many grand
buildings mixed with more modern penitentiary-
style pseudo-ecological monstrosities, some of

which were beautiful for that very reason. No lovelier place among the creations of human hand to this impressionable mind than the square between the Allen Building and Shryock Auditorium. The size of this square was enhanced when the Old Main Building was burned to the ground during the campus riots of the Decades of Tumult in the late 20th. The fountain of the imp holding an umbrella leaves a mark. The rooms where I had sat as a student were now rooms wherein I held forth, teetering upon the narrow fence-line of experience of two full years teaching in Hampton. Thompson Lake, the park bench, Cherry Street, Illinois Avenue, Devil's Kitchen, and the Devil's Stand Table. Lots of devils, and angels, in southern Illinois.

Virginia, Hampton, where I was between Texas and going to Southern Illinois the second time. Another world. From Chicagoland to the edge of the nation. The ocean ever present even when out of view. Never more than a few miles from it for months at a time. Not better air. Different. Heavier but not too heavy to breathe. Polluted by nature and by man, and in the violent meeting of the two. Crabbing, the thick powdery stench hanging and floating with the fog off the harbor. A nauseating pall to which the locals seemed immune if not fond. I got used to it, but never loved it. The endless bridges and flowages and tidal waterways and one way streets and neighborhoods like Buckroe and Phoebus. Accents mixing the old Old South with even older British Isles. Crab cakes. Fritters. Outrageously good cooking at the school. Soul food. Can a white boy safely adore it forty years past without someone calling for his statue to be razed? Pretty sure it's OK. Hampton. I had no idea how fantastic it was much of the time. HI really deserves its own volume. Nuff said. I learned new phrases such as "fell out" and "throw down" and "lunchin" -- most of which are, today in 2020, unintelligible to anyone of any color.

"There is no frozen language," as Jane Francis once mused.

New York: Alfred University. You might think you know small. And know it you might. How could I know, stranger? Though there were smaller towns in the county, the wee burg of Alfred, New York was a smudge. Smashed between two steep worn out pine studded ridges, cold enough all the year that air conditioning seemed a bit silly. Snow from September to May, but with lots of variation during that long season of "sinter"--from green grass poking through the February tease to days without power and subzero in April. Chairs were busted up and burned. One cafe, one Shurfine grocery store (or drive 10 miles to the A&P). One part time doctor who genuinely seemed to hate people and particularly patients. Part time police that moved the car once in a while. Hearty and hardy emergency personnel, all volunteer. A school of grand private tradition, crumbling buildings mixed with late masterpieces such as Howell Hall and Steinham Castle. A towering carillon, ringing out across the valley and up it toward Wellsville and down the watershed all the way past Almond to Hornell. Across and down over the ridge, Andover, a town that made Alfred look like a city. Poverty coexisting with a school for the wealthy and the wise. Ceramics, both artistic and of the engineered sort. Superconductivity and glass blowing all on the same acres. Flourishing arts, music, and rabid desperate constant fundraising as the forces of the world sought, ever sought, to shut the Trojans down. Four years I taught there, and at the time and my style and that place were a good mix. My "tenure was inevitable," said the Dean. Why not stay? Just too far from home, when home was still Illinois.

Home may be the place that you were born but it might also become the place you spend most of your life. Now, for me, that would be:

Kentucky, Morehead A sober, distant, unconnected assessment of Morehead would simply call it Alfred after a good meal. If I'd been drugged (more than I already was) and dropped from Alfred into eastern Kentucky, there would not be much in the terrain and foliage to indicate much of a trip. Still, Morehead the town had a striking effect because of its relatively huge size. All the lights! Restaurants! Look, humans! Walmart! The lights the lights! More than 1000 people. Damn! Plus, a splendid university helping to help it all happen. Eastern Kentucky. Like southern Illinois and western New York, a university surrounded by struggle and deprivation mixed with industrious production mixed with the usual amounts of exploitation. People with a helluva lot living 200 yards from people with next to nothing. Which family is most happy might be hard to tell, though.

Used to be, in Morehead, which is now my home by sheer momentum and time, a person could be walking on the sidewalk on Main Street, nowhere near a cross walk, and just THINK about crossing the road--and traffic would stop. People looked after each other in strange ways here. Even in Alfred this was not true all of the time, because many of the drivers grew up in metro NYC and thirsted for blood. Alas, even in sanguine Morehead, this freedom to walk uncrushed is going. Painted crosswalks have become necessary, with very large rubber-poled signs in the road beggin' drivers not to kill walkers, replacing the full-coverage courtesy that used to reign in this fine burg. Depends on the driver now. Just don't bet on making it.

Among my quaint notices from the early days in Morehead: the unforgettable graffiti (or was it?) Some on that later.

Perhaps all teachers can locate their strongest influences in the teachers they worked with as student and colleague along the way. I had so many good teachers that to leave any one of them off the list would be naturally and entirely excusably unfair. Those quoted above somewhere in this whiskered missive are a signal of the sorts of things that helped me to decide what to do when moments arose requiring one to have answers.

August 4, 2020

Ron Havelka, 6th grade teacher of who knows what, saying way too often:

"Awwwwwright."

Usually before hitching up his sagging belt and dispensing justice, which was why he said it so often. Havelka, along with my mother, was fond of saying, "wipe that smile off your face."

All that got me to doing was wondering if a smile was like jelly (good) that needed finishing, or more like mud (actual dirt plus water) that needed cleaning.

Huh.

Many many many many colleagues, fellow students, teachers of mine, and random speakers victimized by my hunger for eavesdropping all said
"Um,"
A LOT.
Even President Obama said it, or one of its many very close cousins,
"Ahhp [unexploded p]"
"Ahhhhm"
"Uhhh"
"Ahhh"[leaning toward uh]
And so on.
I bring up what some would pass off as verbal silage in this hallowed spot of my memoirs because even these verbal boogers (aka vocalized pauses, etc.) did influence me greatly. They influenced me NOT ever to say such stupid shit, uh, as long as I can help it. There was a point where one could be driven mad by hearing it so often, but shifting the view to one of pity and understanding helps greatly, as one would listen to wails in an infirmary.

Lo! the years since 1964, as often as I took the opportunity to speak in classrooms, I said some stupid shit. No doubt. Sometimes I got feedback that was helpful, but most times, as I recall to the best of my eroding ability, people just let it slide. Too tired, I guess, to call a moron by his name.

Not so Marvin Kleinau. He had no trouble telling me, when it really began to matter, that I was capable of speaking stupidly. Though fully convinced by lack of sufficient sanction and negative feedback prior to age 19 that I was in fact witty by nature, Professor Marvin Kleinau noted with brevity, kindly vigor, and a touch of serious scorn that he could conjure simply by relaxing his God-given regal face,

"You are speaking stupidly."

There was no time to react or refute or defend. There was time only to reword, restate, and recover. He was right, you see, and to that there is little one can debate, as much as pride and face might wish. His observation had advice poetically woven into its text, and guidance, and a bit of a warning that said, "this is the classroom; stupid is not invited."

Hence, I tried in my moments of greatest sober and minimal satiation in meetings, classes, and to myself, allowing for the full range poetry requires, NOT to sound stupid. Win some, lose some, etc.

Did the Odyssey simply stream out of Homer's mouth into magnificent song? If he had breathed fewer times per minute, how might his verses have been affected? This has something to do with something but I am not sure what.

Witty isn't always wonderful. Sometimes the teacher has to be the master while also letting the student win. Thus, to them, is borne the value of their voices and speech melody to make subtle qualifications to reactions, say, to poetry.

I once wrote a piece called "The Poet Laurie Ate," filled brim-level with such nonsense as feet being Longfellow's and such. Poetry professor Dr. Judy Little read it with some other student work aloud in class, and remarked with unusual vimicity, "why that's entirely clever!" The words were nice, but the melody said, "and this is poetry class, remember? Screw clever." Praise fainted by music. Memories of THAT taught me to deliver, as a teacher, both levels of response: the proper, civil language and what I really thought (in its most subtle intervallics) in order to remain useful and employed.

See? Teachers are teaching about teaching while teaching what it is they are supposed to teach.

No one is 100% all of the time and there is no doubt that my vigor and focus ebbed during waves of nature naturing hard and working me over through decades of life. If you, dear reader, noticed my brain in particularly unshaven condition on a day or two (or more), my apologies. Even beginning to explain here or there why I was running on autopilot would have taken more time than it was worth and have solved nothing. Broken arms (visible) and pending childbirths (phone at elbow) aside, I chose to remain mysterious, reaching way back to tales about communication.

A few examples became useful:

In the course I taught to more students than any other, Conflict & Communication, the paradox of winning and yet losing seemed timely for mention in each semester.

When I was a wee lad, probably in the mid-low single digits, in our neighborhood kids played in one another's yards all of the time. There might be 3 or 4 families represented in one yard, totaling a dozen kids at times. One day the crowd was a bit smaller, and the "big kids" were tolerating the presence of the wee ones. My older brother Ken and his best friend Jimmy M. were having an argument over something and suddenly it got physical. Now, here is the juicy part, which I hope is true because it is so juicy: After tussling with the usual scary ergs of young wolves, Ken gained the top and stayed there, pinning his friend to the ground. It could just as well have gone the other way, but that's how it went. Ken was victorious. And yet, dominating as he did, pinning his friend to the ground, rightfully able to claim victory, his face had something odd going on when I looked at it.

He was crying.

Lesson? When you win by beating someone down, you haven't won if that person is your friend...

Students never seemed to have trouble understanding that story, or

1. they didn't know what the fuck I was talking about but were being polite
or

2. they got it because it is juvenile and beyond easy to comprehend
and

3. they already effing knew that.

In any case, that is probably the earliest, most-likely mostly true story from my life that I shared with students. All of the other crap above here is getting rolled out fresh for you now. Aren't you lucky?

Sorry if my sarcasm bone is dry today. The end of civilization (sic) is distracting and if it were not for Jane Francis, I'd probably stop this foolishness right now:
"An average fly weighs less than a gram but can ruin an entire donut," she wrote once, on a postcard while she was visiting a friend who was in jail.

Things people have said stick in the head even when one does not know who said them. Case in point: graffiti. On the way to campus the very first day in Morehead I was stopped on Main St at University Boulevard at a red light. In those days, aluminum control boxes could be found affixed to the light poles, about the size of a large, smooth call box. Someone found the door of the control box at UB and Main the perfect canvas for these carefully hand-printed words:

"JESUS IS LARD."

With no traffic behind me, luck leant me a second to think (yes, I was early to campus) and the words began to work their magic. Richard Lanigan, where are you when someone needs you?

Was "Lard" a misspelling? Or an accurate depiction of a person's accent? Or a comment on JC in contrast to pig fat--an equation, one might say? If a misspelling, then a common and unremarkable phrase.

If dialect, an impressive use of the Roman alphabet to present subtle features.
If a metaphor equating Our Lord (sic) with porcine renderings, well, what kind of city have I moved into and what class of graffiti is this? That last interpretation got me thinking I'd landed in some sort of Appalachian Pompeii. This story was useful at all levels in classes, wherever the syntagm and the paradigm got to jamming.

Another interesting message of local flavor, raising the question "mistake or wit?"
was a billboard with a feature so obvious that I, of course, had missed it for months, driving past at least once a day. Locally the Ben Franklin

stores still existed, enough to make posting two billboards in one county a worthwhile investment. Here's how I thought the sign read the first 150 times I drove past it:

B E N F R A N K L I N: Our Area's Most Unusual Store."

But what it really said, (and it took Illinoisan visitor Lisa Modaff to point it out while driving by the very first time), was this:

B E N F R A N K L I N: Our Area's Most UNsual Store."

"Unsual?" she asked from the back seat, expecting that we knew and could explain. (I may have shared the lard story with her).
"What?"
"That sign, most UNsual store? Is that a word?"
"It is now," somebody else noted dryly.
Mistake? Witty coinage?
If it were a mistake, it was made twice, as the very same billboard, a monster in size and color, appeared in the southern part of the county, too. But I like to think it was wit. What could accomplish any better the meaning of the term than to spell "unusual" as "unsual?" Also, the assonance with "sensual" and "unsual" becomes operative in some very makeup-

counter sorts of ways... Another useful
example for this professor, during discussions of
local flavor, the ambiguity of "errors," and
paradigmatic shifts leading to different
meanings for words.

August 5, 2020

While politicians and their huge armies of messagers are busy devising ways to make evil the face of the Other, we once again take time to reflect on what can be remembered (and remembered as remembered) about the last 40 years posing as a teacher.

The Plan

...was that I would study for 4 years and become a high school English teacher, flavoring the lives of eager young minds with great literature plus a bit of writing direction tossed into the salad. Ahhh, youth. College took care of that.

The exact moment when I decided "I have to get the f out of here," was in EDUC 210 (sic), in the Education Building (a funny name on a campus with so many inventive names, like Pulliam Hall, and Morris Library). The professor was that day speaking about a federal law that stipulated categorization of students into classes of disability. That was the last straw. Absolutely everyone is handicapped, the way I saw it (and see it.) And quite a few people who are so-defined are held back not by their capacity but by their definition. That last straw snapped a camel weighted by disappointing field visits to classrooms in middle and high schools (watching people who were tired of their jobs work as zookeepers) and the realization that Parents would be in the mix. All of this sent me running to the SIU-C Communication Building in search of rescue.

To honor RP Hibbs, "I teach college students about speech communication."

about articulatory phonetics and the organs that make it real

about phonemes and morphemes and emes of all kinds

about what the book says under Fallacies

about what it says under Rhetoric about how the best evidence that communication and speech are vital to our health:

alone

226

in a pair
in a group
in any endeavor

The only career that does not require adept speech communication is hermit. And, of course, we'll never hear about them.

Maybe RP Hibbs had a screw or two loose, because he would also often wonder "why Speech Communication? Isn't all speech communication?" never realizing that maybe all communication was not speech, to some. But I agreed with him and still do. The field's name has changed. One of the words had to go and, sadly, it was speech: the only college major protected in the US Constitution.

Teaching college has been a gas. My teachers from grade school through PhD school provided nearly every worthwhile thing I had to offer in 5 states across 40 years. To all of them, living and gone, thank you. And to the students who endured my endless productions in speech and in spectacle (and occasionally in music), who trusted me to recommend them to careers, who decided to stay and to finish, to all who leapt into the world wearing a coat with a few threads of mine, Thank You.

As for "f-you's", I don't have any. For I am very sure that any and every
displeasantry purported or realized from others was duly answered by my own, one way or another.

EPILOGUE

August 17, 2020

Professors who have made it this far in my modest memoirs are probably wondering where all of the professor stuff in my story has gone. Why no descriptions of the Endless Boring Meetings (EBM's), convocations, commencements, committees, curriculum revisions (endless), crusades for publication, tenure review and academic politics that comprise the plots of so many good murder novels? Because little or none of that really has anything to do with teaching.
I taught in spite of all of that, not because of it.
Morehead State University opens Fall classes amid the pandemic today.
Am I sorry not to be there? You can guess...The buzzing mania of higher ed will endure without this wee graying Sisyphus' noisemaking. Adieu and best to all still pushing that stone up that hill.

JV Modaff, Morehead Kentucky